LINKS

Inspired BEAD and WIRE Jewelry Creations

BY JEAN YATES

NORTH LIGHT BOOKS
CINCINNATI, OHIO

ABOUT THE AUTHOR

Jean Yates is an inventive and unique designer whose background as an English major adds a special twist to her work. Her designs have been featured in magazines such as *BeadStyle, Beadwork, Belle Armoire's Salon, Simply Beads, Stringing* and *Australian Beading.* Jean's work has appeared in books as well, including *The Little Box of Beaded Bracelets and Earrings, The Little Box of Beaded Necklaces and Earrings, Best of BeadStyle: Discover Beading, BeadStyle's Easy Beading: Vol. 3* and *BeadStyle's Easy Beading: Vol. 4.* Her work also appeared on PBS's *Beads Baubles and Jewels.*

At home with her family and husband, Jean likes to relax by making jewelry. Visit her online at www.prettykittydogmoonjewelry.com.

Photograph of Jean Yates by her son, James Ian Yates

12 11 10 09 08   5 4 3 2 1

Library of Congress Cataloging-in-Publication Data

Yates, Jean, 1951-
  Links : inspired bead and wire jewelry creations / Jean Yates. -- 1st ed.
    p. cm.
  Includes index.
  ISBN 978-1-60061-016-5
  1. Jewelry making. 2. Beadwork. 3. Wire craft. I. Title.
  TT212.Y37 2008
  745.594'2--dc22
                      2007027432

Distributed in Canada by Fraser Direct
100 Armstrong Avenue
Georgetown, ON, Canada L7G 5S4
Tel: (905) 877-4411

Distributed in the U.K. and Europe by David & Charles
Brunel House, Newton Abbot, Devon, TQ12 4PU, England
Tel: (+44) 1626 323200, Fax: (+44) 1626 323319
E-mail: postmaster@davidandcharles.co.uk

Distributed in Australia by Capricorn Link
P.O. Box 704, South Windsor, NSW 2756 Australia
Tel: (02) 4577-3555

Editors: Jessica Gordon and Jennifer Claydon
Cover Designer: Kim Howes
Interior Designer/Art Director: Cheryl Mathauer
Production Coordinator: Greg Nock
Photographers: Christine Polomsky,
Tim Grondin and Al Parrish
Stylist: Jan Nickum

fw
F+W PUBLICATIONS, INC.
www.fwbookstore.com

METRIC CONVERSION CHART

to convert	to	multiply by
Inches	Centimeters	2.54
Centimeters	Inches	0.4
Feet	Centimeters	30.5
Centimeters	Feet	0.03
Yards	Meters	0.9
Meters	Yards	1.1
Sq. Inches	Sq. Centimeters	6.45
Sq. Centimeters	Sq. Inches	0.16
Sq. Feet	Sq. Meters	0.09
Sq. Meters	Sq. Feet	10.8
Sq. Yards	Sq. Meters	0.8
Sq. Meters	Sq. Yards	1.2
Pounds	Kilograms	0.45
Kilograms	Pounds	2.2
Ounces	Grams	28.3
Grams	Ounces	0.035

DEDICATION

Jim. Jim! Jim! Jim! Jim: It's always Jim. I love Jim! This book is for *Jim Yates*, my superwonderful husband!

ACKNOWLEDGMENTS

If not for my husband, Jim, I never would have gotten my very first tools and beads. When I didn't know a head pin from an eye pin, he would bring home all sorts of things from local craft stores for me. Thank you, Jim. You fed my desire to create at the expense of your own, encouraging me every day. You admired my work! You rule!

If not for Margot Potter, Bead Queen of the Universe™, friend, confidante and ever-generous guide in the sometimes confusing, yet always fascinating, Brave New World of beading books, I would not have been given the opportunity to present my book idea to North Light. Thank you, Margot. I am sure the words "Help! What do I do now?" are still reverberating in your ears, yet you were always illuminating and patient! I love you for that! I am in your debt for so much, it's ridiculous.

If not for my dear friend Elizabeth Gerlach, who faithfully held onto my manuscript and instructions as I worked away for months before I began sending North Light my book, I would potentially have lost important, irreplaceable information. That is a true and good pal. Thank you, Elizabeth. I owe you big time. Your bracelet is on its way!

If not for Aislyn of Urban Maille, I never would have learned how to make chain maille. She is so inspiring and so talented, it's downright dazzling. Thank you, Aislyn, straight from my heart. You give so much to all of us. And thank you for not teasing me too much for replacing so many tools!

If not for Paul Yates, our film director nephew, who accompanied me to Ohio for the book shoot, cheerfully drove me everywhere, entertained everyone in his intelligent way and got us both dinner at the grocery store at night, I might have accidentally eaten some meat, or worse, done something uncool, which I am apt to do. Thank you, Paul—you are unfazeable.

If not for Jessica Gordon, superb editor for North Light, and a teacher and writer as well, I would not have gotten to first base with my book. She made the knockout presentation to end all presentations! Then she figuratively held my hand through a large part of the jewelry creating process and my visit to Ohio. She teamed up at that point with the amazing Jennifer Claydon. Together they brought this book to life.

If not for Jennifer, I could quite possibly still be wandering around Ohio in a haze. Jennifer gets the job done! She had all my jewelry and components laid out for me, and all my instructions typed up when I arrived. She has the eye of an artist. She makes lampwork, she spins and knits what are essentially art pieces in wool, silk and cashmere, and she makes her own jewelry. She is an incredible person!

Together, these two made up my cheerful, charming, multi-talented dream team. I couldn't have wished for anything better. Thank you both so much—you are superb at what you do. I am so lucky I got you, Double Js! I am very grateful!

Finally, a huge hug and a thank you to Christine Polomsky, my photographer. You are a remarkable, cool person who thinks the shots out elegantly and perfectly in advance. You are truly a great photographer. And you have the best laugh I have ever heard!

Thanks to the great group at North Light, those I had the chance to meet and those I did not, who worked on this book to make it so lovely!

Thank you to my dear friends and interview participants. Each of you looked way inside and brought such wonderful, illuminating contributions to *Links*. I owe you a huge debt.

To Jamie, you are flat out wonderful!

To Lisa Kan, an artist I am just getting to know better, you are a delight to have in my life!

To Green Girl Studios, Redside Designs and to Dakota Stones, thank you for your generosity! And thank you to Greg Ogden of Green Girl Studios for explaining the composition of shibuichi to me.

To Damien Rice, I am consistently amazed at how you transport me.

To Jennifer Dangerfield, you are an extraordinary artist whom I love!

To Rae, love and thanks for helping me to understand mandalas.

To Bronwyn Evans, thanks for the great refresher course on PMC.

To my children and family, of course, I can do it—with your love.

Special thanks and love to Emma, Kim and Kate! You came through for Dylan and our whole family at a very important time. We will always love you for this.

CONTENTS

INTRODUCTION 6
MATERIALS 8
TECHNIQUES 14

FAMILY AND FRIENDS 20
Charming Teacup Bracelet 22

Mother's Love Pin and Choker 24

Elegant Underwater Earrings 26

Alice's Cosmopolitan Necklace 28

Caveman Key Ring 30

Hip Chicks Earrings 32

Roses for Elizabeth Bracelet 34

Treasured Friends Necklace 38

Nancy's Dancing Pearls Bracelet 40

NATURE 42
Petals and Vines Bracelet and Earrings 44

Portrait of Nature Necklace 48

Magnificent Mineral Lariat 50

Turning Leaf Earrings 52

Citrus Gumdrop Necklace 56

Spiral Earrings 58

Delicate Necklace 60

Blooming Chain Maille Earrings 62

Trinity Spiral Necklace 64

Spice Market Earrings 66

Fairy in the Garden Necklace 68

Golden Hues Bracelet and Earrings 70

Indian Summer Necklace 72

BEAD BOX 74

Two Serendipitous Bracelets 76

Red Planet Necklace 80

Naughty and Nice Bracelet 82

Sara Crewe Charm Bracelet 84

Gigi Bracelet 88

Pictograph Bracelet 90

Mandala Earrings 94

Edward the Sheep Bracelet 96

Sleek Squares Bracelet 98

Diamond Choker 102

Art House Bracelet 104

Ancient Armor Bracelet 106

Trio of Sparkling Earrings 110

COLOR 114

Rainbow Ruffles Necklace 116

Sun and Shadow Necklace 118

Electric Purple Necklace 120

RESOURCES 124
INDEX 126

INTRODUCTION

What is a link?

A link is a connection, whether it is a thought, a collection of letters that make a word, an Internet address or an expression of an attachment between people. A link has all sorts of connotations, but they all have one thing in common: A link is pretty worthless without something going before it and something following it. To make sense, it must be connected in some manner.

Imagine looking at one jump ring lying in front of you, all by itself. You would see instantly that you couldn't accomplish much with just that one. However, take that ring, add a shiny pile more, and with a little knowledge and the right tools, there you'd be, flashing a fantastic piece of jewelry!

I believe that something very special takes place with good design in jewelry. If you want to design original jewelry that tells your story, you have to look inside yourself. I will teach you methods to kick-start your personal links and connections. You can draw creative inspiration from even the most mundane objects and the most unlikely thoughts that float into your head. Examine and analyze color, materials, space (and lack of it), shapes and techniques. Or draw on other sources of inspiration, including memories, songs and books. I particularly get inspired by songs. I've spent days driving around in my car listening to music, only to come home with song lyrics in my head, racing to make a necklace.

Every piece of jewelry in this book has a story. I will tell you what I was thinking about when I designed each piece, with the hope that this will inspire you to get excited about designs of your own. I will also offer you Creative Challenges to help you find inspiration all around you. Look for the Creative Connection feature for thoughts on inspiration and creativity from some of my favorite creative people.

I must admit I love fine beads, chains and all sorts of odds and ends. I have used the Internet to locate some of the finest. However, if you cannot replicate what I make in this book exactly, please realize that this is intended as a guide for what dwells in your own heart, and not in mine. By following your heart as you design your own jewelry, and staying true to yourself and your own spirit, you will never stray far from making perfectly beautiful, totally unique, storytelling jewelry of your own.

MATERIALS

Sometimes when I design, I'm driven by the great materials I discover. They alone can be my source of inspiration. We are fortunate right now to be able to comb the world, through magazines and the Internet, for materials from all sorts of sources. Choose the right materials and you will see the most remarkable creations emerge!

TOOLS

Who doesn't remember her first set of tools? My first jewelry-making tools were a Christmas present from my husband, Jim. They served me well, but when I was ready to try chain maille, that first set was not up to the task, so I upgraded. Always use the right tool for the job: It will make your jewelry more durable and your life much easier. Make sure your tools have the right fit and tension for you. You never want pain to stop you when inspiration strikes!

Round-Nose or Rosary Pliers have round, graduated tips and are used for a multitude of purposes, including wire wrapping beads, dangles and charms. I prefer pliers with small tips because they let me make small loops when I am wire wrapping. If you plan to work with memory wire, you will need a second pair of round-nose pliers made specifically for working with memory wire.

Chain-Nose Pliers have narrow, flat tips and are essential when dealing with jump rings. These are a staple in both my chain maille toolbox and my regular jewelry design toolbox.

Flat-Nose Pliers are similar to chain-nose pliers, but have wider, flatter tips. This makes them great for really getting a grip on wire and other items, as well as for working with sturdy items such as leather crimps.

Bent-Nose Pliers have angled tips that make them very useful for getting into hard-to-reach places, such as pushing in the cut end of a wire wrap. I also find these invaluable when working with jump rings, especially when working chain maille. Some people prefer to use two pairs of chain-nose pliers to work with jump rings instead of my preference for a pair of chain-nose and a pair of bent-nose pliers. Experiment and use the tools that work best for you.

Round-Nose Pliers

Round-Nose Pliers for Memory Wire

Chain-Nose Pliers

Flat-Nose Pliers

Bent-Nose Pliers

8

TIP

Keep your chain maille tools as free of scratches as possible, because sterling silver jump rings show marks easily. Use an emery board to smooth out any nicks or scratches on the tips of your pliers.

Flush Cutters have two very sharp blades capable of cutting metal. I have three pairs of cutters: one for memory wire, one for beading wire and one for everything else. When cutting memory wire, use flush cutters made exclusively for cutting memory wire and protect your eyes with safety glasses or goggles. The coating on beading wire also requires a special pair of flush cutters, so buy a pair made for beading wire. For your general-purpose flush cutters, a high quality pair is invaluable, because it will cut wire cleanly and give your work a more finished look.

Wire Straighteners have wide, flat, nylon-padded tips. Pulling a length of wire or the shaft of a head pin through the closed tips of the wire straighteners will both straighten the wire and work-harden it. These are great for straightening out spooled wire that has a curve to it, or for neatening up any wire or head pins that are less than perfect.

Scissors may be a tool you'd be surprised to find in a jewelry kit, but they are an important addition to anyone's toolbox, especially for cutting ribbon, leather and suede, or rubber tubing. Do not to use your scissors on wire, though, or you'll just ruin them!

Measuring Tape or a Ruler will help you size your jewelry. I've included some standard measurements here for you, but I recommend sizing your jewelry to your own taste.

Flush Cutters

Flush Cutters
for Memory Wire

STANDARD SIZES

BRACELETS	NECKLACES
6½" (17cm) = very small	14" (36cm) = petite choker length
7" (18cm) = small	16" (41cm) = choker length
7½" (19cm) = average	18" (46cm) = princess length, a classic length for pearls
8" (20cm) = average to large	20" (51cm) = matinee length, perfect over a turtleneck

Wire Straighteners

Ruler

Scissors

Flush Cutters
for Beading Wire

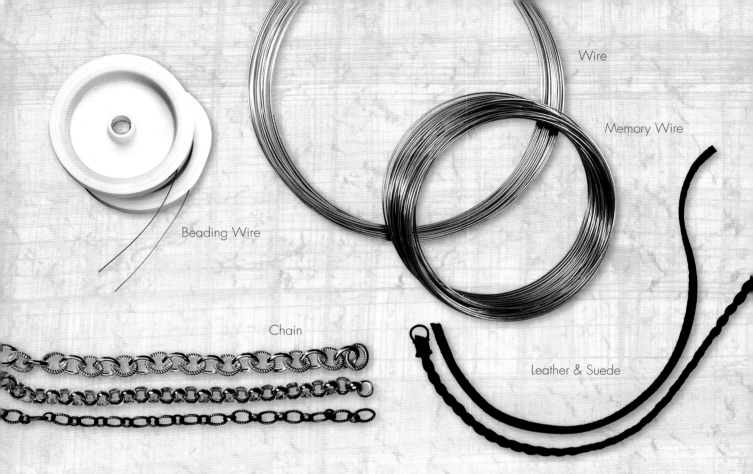

Wire

Memory Wire

Beading Wire

Chain

Leather & Suede

STRINGING MATERIALS

Stringing materials are the foundation of a piece of jewelry. I like to achieve unique effects by combining different stringing materials. Try experimenting with new stringing materials—you'll be surprised at the effect it will have on your jewelry!

Beading Wire is composed of cabled strands of stainless steel wire coated in nylon. The higher the strand count of the wire, the stronger and more flexible the wire . I recommend 49-strand wire for its durability. Beading wire also comes in different diameters. When creating jewelry, use the thickest beading wire that will fit through your beads. This will make your jewelry as strong as possible. I consider .019" (.48mm) beading wire a good all-purpose beading wire.

10

Chain comes in a variety of metals, colors and styles, from fine to ultra-heavy. I like to use chain as the base of a design, adding beads and charms as I go, but chain can also be a great decorative accent to a piece. Try combining different types of chain in your jewelry for a new twist on a design.

Wire is available in several different thicknesses, or gauges. The higher a wire's gauge number, the thinner the wire. Again, I recommend using the thickest wire that will fit through your beads for strong, long-lasting jewelry. Wire is one of my favorite stringing materials because I love to wire wrap. I find creating a strand of wire-wrapped beads incredibly magical.

Memory Wire is a rigid wire that has been wound into a coil shape. It comes in bracelet, necklace and ring sizes. I love the structure memory wire gives to a piece of jewelry. Always use tools designed for memory wire when you are using it, though, or you'll ruin your tools.

Leather and Suede can also be used in jewelry when they have been cut down into laces. Leather and suede both have great texture and can give a design an updated look. Try replacing a traditional stringing material with leather or suede for a totally different appearance.

FINDINGS

Findings, also known as components, are used to attach the different elements of a design. Because findings are responsible for holding your jewelry together, it is important to use high-quality items. You don't want to discover too late that your bracelet isn't strong enough to hold together while you're hanging onto the strap on the subway! There are many innovative products on the market today, so try different styles of findings to discover what works best for you and your style of jewelry design.

Crimp Tubes

Crimp Tubes are used to secure beading wire to a clasp and are also available in larger sizes for thick stringing materials, such as ribbon or leather. I prefer Twisted Tornado Crimps because they will hold a piece of jewelry securely without using a special tool. Regular crimp tubes require a special crimping tool to properly close them. It is essential that you crimp properly. If you don't, your jewelry will not have a chance of sticking around.

Jump Rings are a quick and easy way of connecting your jewelry components. If you close the ring securely and properly, the ring appears to be almost smooth. Not only are jump rings great for attaching charms and clasps, but they are also used to make chain maille. When selecting jump rings for chain maille, take the inner diameter of the rings into account, because it will play an important role in the finished look of your piece. For most of my jump ring needs, I use Urban Maille.

Jump Rings

Clasps are the exclamation point at the end of the expressive statement you have made. Nothing can make or break a jewelry design quicker than the clasp. Try using a special clasp as a starting point for a design, or put a gorgeous clasp front and center on a necklace, instead of hiding it in the back. A great clasp will more than make up for a higher cost with its dramatic impact.

Head Pins are short pieces of wire with a stopper on one end, and they come in many different gauges and lengths. I like longer head pins because I get more control when I wire wrap. Try head pins with inlaid or dangling stones, handmade head pins with decorations on them and head pins with contrasting color for a special touch in your designs.

Multi-Strand Attachments come in a variety of forms, from clasps for necklaces and bracelets to chandeliers for earrings. Multi-strand attachments allow you to play with balance, color, placement and your own inventive skills.

Clasps

Multi-Strand Attachments

Head Pins

BEADS AND SUNDRIES

Even if you start slowly, gingerly putting one foot into the world of beads, you will be amazed by the array of treasures available for your creations. You can take your designs in any direction you like with the beads, crystals and gemstones offered to you. You become a great explorer just by strolling into your local bead store—your own personal finds will turn into the beginning of a collection that will spark your creativity and incite your imagination every time you look at it!

Gemstone and Semi-Precious Beads

Other Natural Beads

Lampwork Beads

Polymer Clay Beads

12

Gemstone and Semi-Precious Beads are available in every color of the rainbow and can be cut into endless shapes and sizes. They can also be dyed, reconstituted or heat treated to create even more variety. One important factor to consider when designing a piece is the hardness of the stone. If you design a bracelet and choose a really soft stone, it could break after you have strung it. If you have any concerns about a stone you are considering, check out the Mohs Scale of Hardness on page 125 to further investigate a gemstone's characteristics.

Other Natural Beads include pearls, mother-of-pearl, shell, bone, amber, wood and lac. The variety of materials we obtain from nature is both fascinating and beautiful. If you are not familiar with these materials, be sure to give them a try. You'll be surprised by how easily they can be combined with more traditional materials.

Lampwork Beads can be made of soft glass, also known as "soda lime" glass, or borosilicate glass, also known as "boro" glass. Lampwork beads are available in all sorts of shapes and sizes. Have you ever played the game where you name ten things you would take if you were stuck on a remote island? I personally would take a helicopter reservation for later that day, and a collection of nine lampwork beads from different great bead artists to study. Some people collect paintings or sculpture. I collect beautiful lampwork. Compared to many other beads, the price for lampwork may seem high, but the time put into them and the design factor of certain beads makes them worthy of being displayed in a gallery. Some are in galleries, in fact.

Polymer Clay Beads are a great addition to your bead box. There are some very talented artists working in polymer clay today, so there are many beautiful beads available for purchase. If you're feeling adventurous, you might even want to try making a few of your own.

TIP

Many other items can also be used in your jewelry designs that you might not think of when you consider traditional jewelry elements. For instance, thin rubber tubing cut into short sections can be used as beads. Buttons are great additions to jewelry. Try adding a wide variety of items to your jewelry designs. You'll be surprised at what you can include when you use a little imagination.

Swarovski Crystal is a staple in my jewelry designs. Swarovski currently creates a huge variety of beautiful products, including crystal beads, pearls and a variety of findings decorated with crystals. I highly recommend taking advantage of all they offer.

Metal Beads come in many forms, from simple spacer beads to elaborate filigree beads. Materials including gold, silver and shibuichi can be used to make metal beads. There are also base metal beads created to resemble more expensive materials.

Antique Beads are available from many different sources these days. I love antique beads because they add something truly unique to a design. Use them as an accent, or base your entire design on them, but either way, try these blasts from the past.

Other Man-Made Beads are available in a wide variety of materials. Several examples are included in this book, such as resin beads, porcelain beads, seed beads and sunstone beads. With so many options, you're sure to find that "special something" to complete your design.

Bead Caps are great little additions to your designs. A beautifully decorated bead cap can add a feminine touch to a design, while a simple bead cap can give your jewelry a contemporary feel. Try experimenting with bead caps of different sizes, too. These can be a great enhancement to your designs.

Charms and Dangles are one of my favorite design elements. If I have a piece of chain, I usually put a charm or a dangle on it! And don't stop at bracelets—dangles and charms are great on necklaces and earrings as well.

Ribbon is a versatile item that can be used as a stringing material or as a decorative item. Little accents of ribbon are entertaining and fun. Make sure you get extra if you really love it, because eventually it will wear out. When it does, you can just add a new piece and start over.

Swarovski Crystal

Metal Beads

Antique Beads

Other Man-made Beads

Bead Caps

Charms and Dangles

Ribbon

13

TECHNIQUES

Before bringing your fabulous creations to life, you'll need to learn the techniques used to craft jewelry. I cannot stress enough how important it is to create well-made, durable jewelry. Get your techniques for all types of jewelry crafting down correctly. You will be the better jewelry maker for it.

WORKING WITH JUMP RINGS

Jump rings are integral to my jewelry designs. Jump rings can be used to hold on a clasp or to make up an entire piece of chain maille jewelry. Proper technique is very important with jump rings, so practice, practice, practice!

Opening and Closing Jump Rings

Learn to open and close jump rings properly before you work with them. If you don't do this correctly, you will have odd little shapes, not neat little rings. But take heart! This is easy to learn.

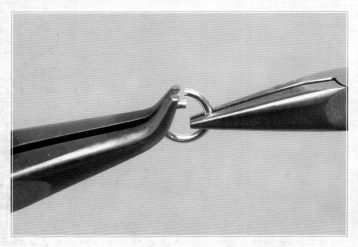

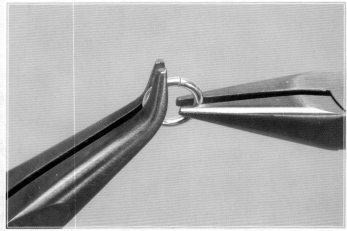

1. Open jump ring

Grasp the jump ring with pliers on both sides of the break. Here, I am using a pair of bent-nose pliers and chain-nose pliers, but two pairs of chain-nose pliers could also be used. To open the ring, keep one pair of pliers stationary and rotate the other pair away from yourself.

2. Close jump ring

To close the jump ring, rotate the pliers in the opposite direction, moving the ends past each other, then back toward each other until they line up cleanly.

Use the same method to open and close a cut loop at the bottom of an ear wire.

Attaching Multiple Jump Rings to the Same Location

Attaching multiple jump rings plays a big part in making chain maille. Many designs look quite complicated, but each is built ring by ring. Use this technique for beautiful results every time.

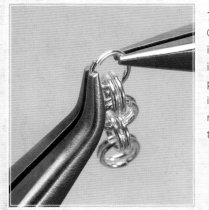

1. Attach first ring

Open a jump ring and slide it into position. When working chain maille patterns, the position of the rings is very important. Make sure the ring is correctly positioned, then close it.

2. Attach second ring

Open a second jump ring. Carefully follow the path of the first jump ring when adding the second jump ring. Close the second jump ring. Repeat if more than two jump rings attach to the same location.

Making a Flower Unit with Jump Rings

I love flower units in chain maille and use them in many ways. When done properly, they add a pretty, feminine touch to your chain maille designs, and their construction makes them very sturdy.

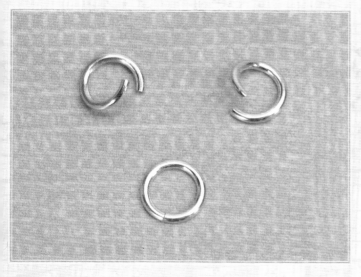

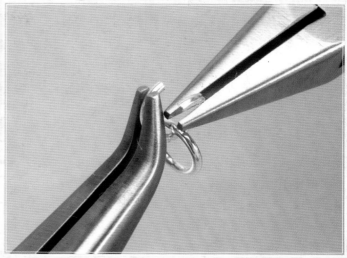

1. Prepare rings
Each flower requires three rings, two open and one closed.

2. Link two rings
Hook an open ring through a closed ring and close.

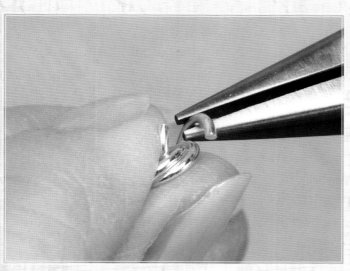

3. Add third ring
Flip the top ring down so it rests on top of the bottom ring. Pinch the two rings together and hook an open ring through both of the connected rings. Close the last ring.

4. Arrange rings
Flip the third ring down to rest on top of the other two so they form a flower.

WIRE WRAPPING

Wire wrapping is a great way to assure your piece isn't going to go anywhere anytime soon. Always use a head pin or wire thick enough to support the beads you are wrapping. For a finished look, make sure the wrapping is neat and consistent, and cut the end so it will not show on the front of the finished piece.

Wire Wrapping on a Head Pin

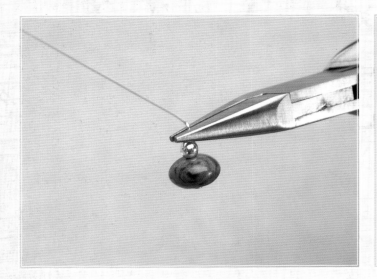

1. Bend wire

Place the bead(s) on a head pin. Grasp the head pin directly over the bead(s) with a pair of chain-nose pliers. Using your fingers, bend the wire over the head of the pliers to a 90° angle.

2. Begin loop

Grasp the head pin at the bend with round-nose pliers. Using your fingers, pull the wire up and over the top of the round-nose pliers.

3. Complete loop

Rotate the pliers until they are positioned as shown, and continue to wrap the head pin around the pliers until a full loop is formed.

4. Add chain (optional)

To wire wrap to a chain, thread the end of the head pin through a link in the chain and push the link up to the loop in the head pin. Use the same method to wrap a beaded head pin to another wire wrap, a charm or any other item.

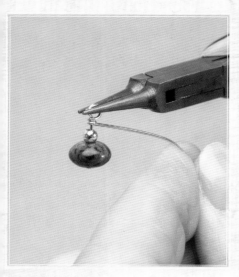

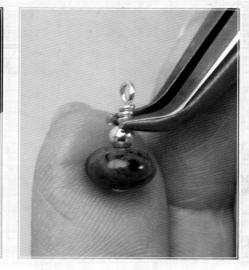

5. Begin coil
While gripping the loop with round-nose pliers, wrap the end of the head pin around the base of the loop with your fingers, working down toward the bead.

6. Cut head pin
Trim the end of the head pin as close to the coil as possible with flush cutters.

7. Tighten wrap
Use bent-nose or chain-nose pliers to push the cut end flush with the rest of the coil.

Wire Wrapping with Wire

There are times when you will find it useful to wrap a bead or a series of beads with connecting wire loops at both ends. I think that a chain of wire-wrapped beads has a very cool look. Wire wrapping is also a sturdy way to attach a clasp. If I ever suspect that jump rings are not going to hold my clasp to a jewelry piece, I opt for wire wrapping.

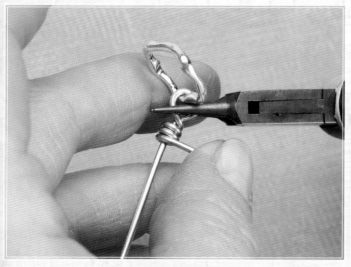

1. Create first wrap
Cut a piece of wire long enough to accommodate the beads to be wrapped plus two long tails to make wrapping easier. Before placing any beads on the wire, follow Steps 1–7 of Wire Wrapping on a Head Pin to close the wire on one end (see Techniques, pages 16–17). If the wire is being used to join two pieces of chain, make sure to place the chain on the loop before closing.

2. Create second wrap
Slide the bead(s) onto the wire and create a second wrap at the other end of the wire, following the same method used for the first wrap.

Bundled Wire Wrap

The appearance of this type of wire wrap is offbeat and free-form. I like this look when I am creating a piece of jewelry with a wilder dimension. You can do this sort of wrap with head pins or cut pieces of wire, but you will need to use a smaller gauge and a longer piece than you would for a traditional wire wrap.

1. Create first coil
Follow Steps 1–5 of Wire Wrapping on a Head Pin to start the bundled wire wrap (see Techniques, pages 16–17).

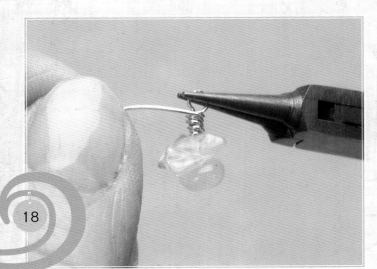

2. Continue wrapping
Once you have wrapped the wire or head pin all the way down to the bead, start a second coil by wrapping up toward the loop.

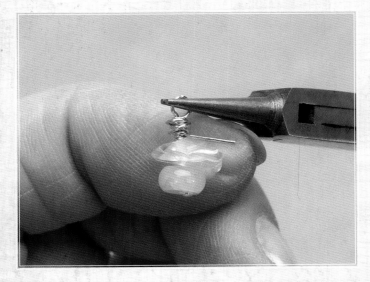

3. Create bundle
After reaching the loop, begin wrapping down toward the bead again. Once the third coil is complete, cut the wire and tighten the last wrap with bent-nose or chain-nose pliers.

ATTACHING A CRIMP TUBE

Crimping is something all beaders must learn to do properly, to ensure the crimp is both attractive and secure. Always use a crimp that is suited to the thickness of your beading wire.

Single Crimp

I choose a single crimp for a piece of jewelry when I want the clasp and the beads close to each other. I also choose the single crimp when the crimps add no design impact to a piece, and the piece does not call for the strength of a double crimp.

1. String crimp and clasp
String beading wire through a crimp tube and clasp. Loop the beading wire back through the crimp tube. Make sure the strands of beading wire are parallel, not crossed.

2. Close crimp
Squeeze the crimp tube closed with chain-nose pliers. String a few beads over both of the pieces of beading wire joined by the crimp tube. Trim the short piece of beading wire.

Double Crimp

I like a double crimp for aesthetic reasons and to hold my jewelry pieces securely. For heavier pieces, two crimps are better than one.

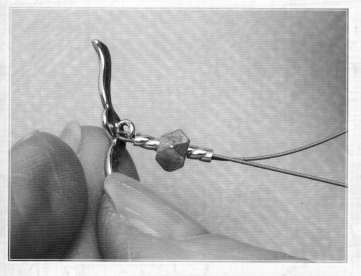

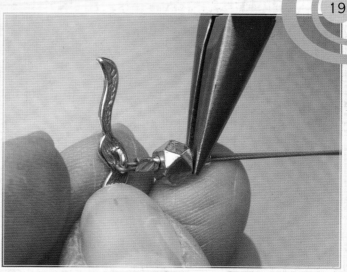

1. Add bead
String beading wire through a crimp tube and clasp. Loop the beading wire back through the crimp tube. Place a bead and a second crimp tube over both pieces of wire.

2. Close crimps
Squeeze both crimp tubes closed with chain-nose pliers. String a few beads over both ends of beading wire and cut off the short end.

FAMILY AND FRIENDS

Your memories can prove to be strong influences in creating meaningful jewelry designs. You can inspire your work by allowing your mind to travel back in time to childhood memories of your family, the way I did with my Elegant Underwater Earrings (page 26). Pausing to dwell on thoughts of friends and loved ones you have fun with now can also influence your work. My jewelry-making friends inspired me to create the Treasured Friends Necklace (page 38). Just as you do when you take a photo, print it out and place it in a special drawer or memory box, you can also freeze precious memories by capturing their essences in your jewelry designs. Your thoughts about the people close to you can be great creative prompts if you are having trouble finding inspiration for a new project.

Every shred of feeling that arises as you wander through your thoughts of family and friends will coax ideas from you. Write your ideas down so they're ready for you when you need them. I have notes all over my calendars, walls (whoops!) and everywhere else I have been on a certain day. If an idea comes to me while I'm cooking dinner, I have a note on a paper towel. If inspiration strikes while I'm typing on the computer, I e-mail myself.

Sometimes it can be a form of meditation for me to think back on someone who is important in my life, and then create a piece of jewelry related to a moment with that person, the way I did when I designed Alice's Cosmopolitan Necklace (page 28). Throughout this chapter, my stories illustrate what inspired each project. You'll also learn how to take your own memories of your friends and family and use them as inspiration when you are designing jewelry.

Charming Teacup Bracelet

MATERIALS

BRACELET

7 lampwork teacup beads (Barbara Becker Simon)

4 4mm Purple Velvet Swarovski rounds

8 4mm Indian Red Swarovski rounds

2 4mm Crystal Moonlight Swarovski rounds

16 4mm Sapphire Swarovski rounds

16 6mm × 9mm Crystal Swarovski teardrops

32 3mm seamless sterling silver beads

7" (18cm) segment of 6mm sterling silver rolo chain

1 sterling silver teapot and spoon toggle clasp (Brightlings Beads)

32 24-gauge sterling silver head pins (for crystal dangles)

7 22-gauge sterling silver head pins (for lampwork teacup dangles)

4 6mm sterling silver jump rings

EARRING VARIATION

2 lampwork teacup beads (Barbara Becker Simon)

4 4mm Crystal Moonlight Swarovski rounds

4 4mm Sapphire Swarovski rounds

4 3mm seamless sterling silver beads

2 matte sterling silver teardrop earring findings (Nina Designs)

4 24-gauge sterling silver head pins (for crystal dangles)

2 22-gauge sterling silver head pins (for lampwork teacup dangles)

TOOLS

round-nose pliers

chain-nose pliers

bent-nose pliers or second pair of chain-nose pliers

flush cutters

The inspiration for this bracelet came from a game I liked to play in college. I would say to a friend, "You are taking a walk in the forest, and you look down and see a cup. What does it look like? First thoughts only, please!" I would then analyze the answer. The first time someone asked me about my cup, I chose a white-and-blue teacup in the classic Blue Onion pattern. If you were to analyze my answer, a teacup might tell you that I see beauty as important and that I am fragile in some ways. The classic china pattern might also tell you that I am traditional. For this bracelet, I chose some wonderful lampwork teacup beads and placed "my" teacup, the white one with blue accents, in the center of the bracelet. I further emphasized my white-and-blue theme with the crystals I used in the bracelet. Then, I created a pair of white-and-blue earrings to match. When you create this bracelet, choose colors that suit you to a "tea!"

1. Attach clasp

Attach the toggle clasp to the end of the chain with two jump rings (see Techniques, page 14). Repeat on the other end.

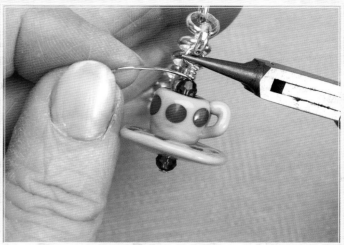

2. Wire wrap teacups

Slide a round crystal bead, a teacup bead and a round crystal bead onto a 22-gauge head pin. Wire wrap this dangle to the fourth link of the chain (see Techniques, pages 16–17). Repeat, adding a teacup dangle to every fourth link in the chain. Wire wrap all of the dangles to the same side of the chain so they will hang properly.

3. Add teardrop dangles

Slide a silver bead and a teardrop bead (with the thin end toward the sterling bead) onto a 24-gauge head pin. Wire wrap this dangle to the first link of the chain. Continue adding teardrop dangles every two links.

4. Add round crystal dangles

Slide a silver bead and a Sapphire round onto a 24-gauge head pin and wire wrap the head pin to the first link, opposite the first teardrop dangle. Repeat every two links to the end of the bracelet.

CHARMING TEACUP EARRINGS

Slide a Crystal Moonlight round, a teacup bead and a Crystal Moonlight round onto a 22-gauge head pin. Wire wrap this dangle to the center hole of the teardrop earring finding (see Techniques, pages 16–17). Slide a seamless silver bead and Sapphire round onto a 24-gauge head pin and wire wrap the beaded head pin to the right of the teacup dangle. Repeat on the left of the teacup dangle. Repeat for the second earring.

23

Mother's Love Pin and Choker

MATERIALS

2 sterling silver heart beads with carpet granulation

1 sterling silver filigree heart bead

7 4mm Amethyst AB Swarovski rounds

1 4mm Olivine Swarovski bicone

2 marcasite flower dangles

2 marcasite flower bud dangles

2 sterling silver heart dangles with granulation

1 sterling silver butterfly dangle

11½" (29cm) length of Rose Mokuba double-faced velvet ribbon (The Ribbon Jar)

6" (15cm) section of sterling silver figure-eight chain

1 sterling silver 5-loop oval pin base

1 7mm × 11mm sterling silver lobster claw clasp

6 24-gauge sterling silver head pins with amethyst dangles

1 22-gauge sterling silver head pin

3 8mm sterling silver jump rings

4 6mm sterling silver jump rings

3 4mm sterling silver jump rings

2 1" (3cm) antiqued silver-plated steel choker clamps (Accessories Susan)

All sterling silver beads and dangles by Nina Designs.

TOOLS

round-nose pliers

chain-nose pliers

flat-nose pliers

bent-nose pliers or second pair of chain-nose pliers

flush cutters

TIP

Attaching the beaded pin to the ribbon choker is, of course, optional. You could simply wear it as a pin instead.

When I was a child, my family spent quite a bit of time at the beach. I remember the times my mother would carefully take a pin out of her jewelry box, singe the end with a match to sterilize it and gently remove a splinter from my finger or toe whenever I got one on the boardwalk. I think of pins when I think of my mother, so to me a pin represents maternal, hands-on love. I designed this pin to commemorate my mother's love for me, my sister and my father. This pin has an old-fashioned style and some attitude. It is not a wimpy pin—there's a lot of action in the dangles! It is glamorous yet playful. Consider other color options for this piece. A black choker would be a classic, elegant look. Or, try switching to pearls or turquoise instead of crystals and amethyst.

1. Attach dangles to left loop

Working from left to right, attach the following dangles to the left-most loop on the pin base: a heart dangle on a 4mm jump ring, an Amethyst AB round on an amethyst head pin, a heart bead with granulations and an Amethyst AB round on an amethyst head pin and a flower dangle on a 6mm jump ring. Wire wrap the beaded head pins to the pin base (see Techniques, pages 16–17).

2. Continue attaching dangles

Working from right to left, repeat Step 1 on the rightmost loop so the dangles on the right loop mirror the dangles on the left loop. Attach a flower bud dangle on a 6mm jump ring to the second loop from the left. Repeat on the second loop from the right.

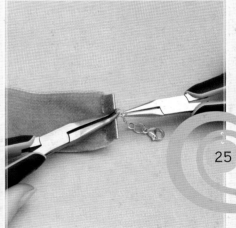

25

3. Attach center dangles

Place the filigree heart bead on an amethyst head pin, add an Amethyst AB round and wire wrap to the center loop. Slide an Olivine bicone and an Amethyst AB round onto an amethyst head pin. Wire wrap this to the center loop, to the right of the filigree heart dangle. Link the butterfly dangle to the top of the Olivine and Amethyst dangle with a 4mm jump ring.

4. Begin to construct choker

Carefully fold the edges of the ribbon in toward the center of the ribbon to match the size of the choker clamp.

5. Attach clasp

Place the ribbon in the choker clamp and crimp down with the flat-nose pliers on both sides, securing the end of the ribbon inside the clamp. Repeat on the other end of the ribbon. Attach three links of chain to one of the choker clamps with an 8mm jump ring. Link the lobster claw clasp to the end of the chain with an 8mm jump ring. Attach a 5" (13cm) length of chain to the other choker clamp with an 8mm jump ring. Slide an Amethyst AB round onto a 22-gauge head pin and wire wrap it to the end of the chain. To finish, attach the pin to the center of the choker.

Elegant Underwater Earrings

MATERIALS

6 6mm × 7mm green freshwater rice pearls

18 3mm Crystal AB Swarovski bicones

6" (15cm) segment of 2.25mm sterling silver double-cable chain

2 sterling silver starfish earring posts (Nina Designs)

2 sterling silver chandelier earring findings (Nina Designs)

24 2½" (6cm) decorative sterling silver head pins

8 4mm sterling silver jump rings

TOOLS

round-nose pliers

chain-nose pliers

bent-nose pliers or second pair of chain-nose pliers

flush cutters

TIP

Do not be afraid to mix up bits and pieces from different findings and components in your designs. Take a piece from this, a bit from that and put it all together the way you want it. The world is your oyster!

My father adored skin diving, an unusual hobby for a man from Nebraska! In fact, to celebrate my parents' tenth wedding anniversary, my father's best friend had a fake newspaper printed up with the headline "Bob Baldridge's Secret to Wedded Bliss: Ten Years Underwater!" I remember going out on our small boat with him when I was a child so he could dive around the pilings of the Atlantic Beach Bridge looking for striped bass. At first, he took a simple spear gun with him, but later he stopped killing fish and instead caught them like butterflies in a net. These Elegant Underwater Earrings are inspired by my father's love of all things aquatic. I started off with starfish earring posts, added chandeliers with delicate swirls reminiscent of seaweed, pearls reflective of the depths of the Atlantic and crystals that glint like sun on the water. When you wear these earrings, they will sway as though pushed by underwater currents.

Here's to my Dad, the best father a kid could have had!

1. Separate components

Remove the chandelier pieces from their ear wires. Put the ear wires aside for another project.

2. Connect chandeliers to posts

Connect a chandelier finding to a starfish earring post with a jump ring. Repeat for the second earring.

3. Attach chains

Cut one 16-link length of double-cable chain, and two 10-link lengths of double-cable chain. Attach the chain pieces to the chandelier finding with jump rings. Place the 16-link chain piece on an end loop of the chandelier finding. Repeat for the second earring, mirroring the chain placement.

27

4. Wire wrap pearls

Place a pearl on a decorative head pin and wire wrap it to the last link of one of the chain pieces (see Techniques, pages 16–17). Repeat, attaching one pearl to each piece of chain.

5. Wire wrap crystals

Wire wrap a Crystal AB bicone to the last link of each chain piece, in front of the pearls. Wire wrap Crystal AB bicones to the left and right sides of the second-to-last link on each chain, for a total of three crystal dangles on each chain.

Alice's Cosmopolitan Necklace

MATERIALS

16 6mm Erinite AB Swarvoski bicones

51 3mm × 4mm white top-drilled pearls

68 2mm × 3mm vermeil hex beads (The Bead Shop)

5 8mm Crystal AB Swarovski rounds

31 6mm faceted amazonite rounds (The Bead Shop)

30 10mm brushed vermeil saucer beads (The Bead Shop)

60 4.5mm Crystal AB gold-tone rondelles (The Bead Shop)

18" (46cm) length of 8mm gold-filled hammered cable chain

2 26" (66cm) strands of .019" (.48mm) 49-strand wire

36" (91cm) piece of 24-gauge gold-filled wire

1 5-strand hook-and-eye vermeil clasp (The Bead Shop)

2 6mm gold-filled jump rings

4 3mm gold-filled crimp tubes

TOOLS

round-nose pliers

chain-nose pliers

bent-nose pliers or second pair of chain-nose pliers

flush cutters

flush cutters for beading wire

TIP

Air and space are just as important to a design as beads, clasps and color. Allowing your designs to breathe sometimes shows off the striking pieces even better. If you are using special beads or stones in your piece, it is very important not to clutter the design by making it too stuffed-up looking. Make sure the balance is exactly what you are looking for.

My older sister, Alice, was born in October, and I was born twenty-three months later, in September. Once a year, for around a month, I get to be only one year younger than Alice. This was a really big deal to me when I was growing up, because I had the mistaken idea that I would eventually catch up to her completely, at which point all my dreams would come true. I spent my life following her around while she spent hers exasperatedly trying to keep me out of her room and away from her friends. Today, Alice is married, has two lovely grown children and is an interior designer in New York City. The necklace I designed for her is centered around the obvious cosmopolitan classic, meant for a classic girl: pearls. I also left a lot of space between the chain and the strung parts of the necklace, because, as Alice reminded me, our mother always said, "When you arrange flowers, you should leave enough space so a butterfly could fly though your arrangement."

1. Attach first strand

Attach one 26" (66cm) length of 49-strand wire to the top loop on the clasp with a crimp tube (see Techniques, page 19).

2. String beads

String beads onto the wire in the following pattern: vermeil hex bead, pearl, vermeil hex bead, pearl, vermeil hex bead, pearl, vermeil hex bead, Erinite AB bicone.

3. Finish first strand

Repeat the beading pattern fifteen more times and end on a series of vermeil hex beads and pearls. Attach the free end of the wire to the top loop of the second piece of the clasp with a crimp tube.

4. Wire wrap second strand

Begin the second strand by linking a piece of gold-filled wire to a 17-link section of chain with a bundled wire wrap (see Techniques, page 18). Slide a Crystal AB round onto the wire and attach an 8-link section of chain to the other end of the wire by creating another bundled wire wrap. Continue joining 8-link sections of chain together with Crystal AB rounds on bundled wraps until the strand has four 8-link sections of chain. Finish the strand with a 17-link section of chain. Connect the beaded chain to the middle loop of each side of the clasp with jump rings.

5. Create third strand

Attach the second 26" (66cm) length of 49-strand wire to the bottom loop of the clasp with a crimp tube. String beads onto the wire, repeating the following pattern seventeen times: amazonite round, gold-tone rondelle, vermeil saucer bead, gold-tone rondelle. End with an amazonite round. To finish, attach the free end of the wire to the bottom loop of the second piece of the clasp with a crimp tube.

Caveman Key Ring

MATERIALS

1 large lampwork art bead (Aardvark Art Glass)

2 6mm green Rococo Miyuki beads (Shepherdess Beads)

1 8mm Kambaba jasper rondelle

1 5mm × 8.5mm sterling silver spacer bead

1 fine silver bead cap (Kate McKinnon)

1 fine silver ring dangle (Kate McKinnon)

1 16mm wavy sterling silver ring (The Bead Shop)

1 26mm sterling silver split ring

8" (20cm) length of 18-gauge sterling silver wire

6" (15cm) length of 20-gauge sterling silver wire

TOOLS

round-nose pliers

chain-nose pliers

bent-nose pliers (optional)

flush cutters

I made this key ring to represent the men in my family because they, collectively, hold the keys to my heart. There is a direct link here from what I chose to make to how I feel when I think about each of them. I love my husband, my children and my grandchildren. They are the key to who I am, and the reason I can free myself to create. I show my delight and love by working with jewelry because I am so happy surrounded by my special family. The lampwork bead used in this key ring is very caveman-ish and elemental. It has a fossil-like pattern on it, as if men have always been this way and share certain masculine characteristics. It is just a flat-out cool bead, and the findings complement the design in a basic and clear way, as if they were all especially made for each other. Just like me and my guys.

TIP

When you have a complex focal bead like this one, keep the other components in the piece simple. That way, the elements of the design won't fight each other for your attention.

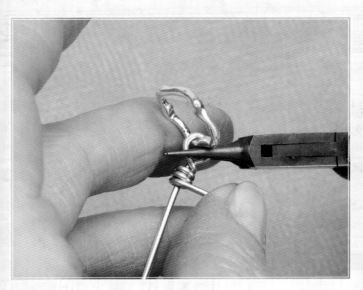

1. Create wire wrap

Wire wrap the 18-gauge wire to the wavy jump ring (see Techniques, page 17).

2. Finish focal section

Attach the split ring to the wavy ring. Slide a Rococo bead, sterling spacer bead, lampwork bead and bead cap onto the wire. Close the end of the wire with a wire wrap.

3. Add dangle

Wire wrap the 20-gauge wire to the silver ring dangle. Slide a Kambaba rondelle and Rococo bead onto the wire. To finish, wire wrap the 20-gauge wire to the 18-gauge wire.

31

CREATIVE CONNECTION

CATHY LYBARGER

Cathy Lybarger is an award-winning lampwork bead artist. The focal bead in this key ring is one of her creations. You can see more of her work at www.aardvarkartglass.net.

Q: What are you most proud of?

A: People tell me my work makes them happy. Sometimes it inspires them to start projects of their own. I like that feeling a lot.

Hip Chicks Earrings

MATERIALS

4 antique trade beads (EJR Beads)

4 1mm × 5.3mm sterling silver spacer beads

4 sterling silver hex beads (The Bead Shop)

4 4.5mm stamped sterling silver cube beads (Nina Designs)

2 Chinese knot earring tops (Nina Designs)

12" (30cm) length of 22-gauge sterling silver wire

2 24-gauge sterling silver head pins

22 18-gauge, ⅛" (3mm) ID cobalt niobium jump rings (The Ring Lord)

12 18-gauge, ⅛" (3mm) ID yellow niobium jump rings (The Ring Lord)

TOOLS

round-nose pliers

chain-nose pliers

bent-nose pliers or second pair of chain-nose pliers

flush cutters

I made these earrings from a bit of "something old, something new" for the women in my family who are all very hip chicks. I wanted to reflect how things come back around time after time. What was once treasured for one reason becomes hip and new, rediscovered. I chose antique trade beads as my "something old" and niobium jump rings for my "something new." I picked blue and yellow rings for the chain maille links to match the beads. I made super-long, linear earrings that I think all of my hip chicks will enjoy. The women in my family are my daughter-in-law, Beth, my husband's daughters, Emily and Abby, my niece, Nina, and my son's fiancée, Kate. You are amazing, each and every one, and I love you! You have accomplished more in your twenties and thirties than I had accomplished by my mid-forties. How did you *do* that?

TIP

Earrings are the perfect way to showcase rare, unique or expensive beads. While one or two beads may get lost in a necklace or bracelet, they can really shine in a pair of earrings!

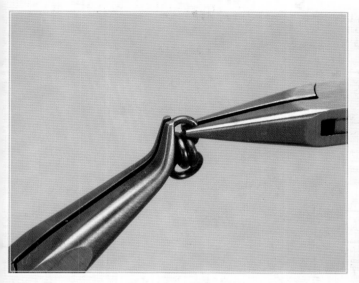

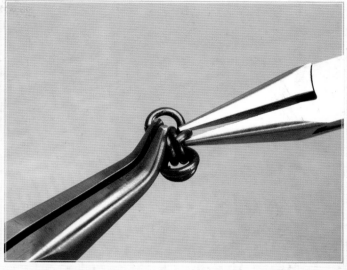

1. Begin building chain

To start the cobalt chain, hook an open jump ring through two closed jump rings and close it. Link a second open jump ring through the two closed jump rings, following the same path as the first ring, and close (see Techniques, page 14).

2. Add to chain

Continue increasing the chain by adding two open rings, one at a time, through the two closed rings just added to the chain. The finished colbalt chain piece should have five 2-ring units.

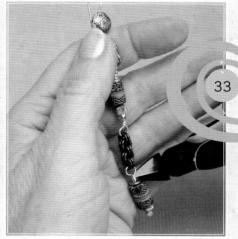

3. Wire wrap chains together

Repeat Steps 1–2 to build a yellow chain with three 2-ring units. Wire wrap a 6" (15cm) piece of 22-gauge wire to the last 2-ring unit of the blue chain (see Techniques, page 17). Slide a hex bead, a stamped cube bead, a trade bead and a spacer bead onto the wire. Wrap the free end of the wire to the end of the yellow chain.

4. Attach ear wire

Link the yellow chain to the earring top with a cobalt jump ring.

5. Finish earring

Slide a hex bead, a stamped cube bead, a trade bead and a silver spacer onto a head pin. Link the beaded head pin to the cobalt chain with a wire wrap. Repeat Steps 1–5 for the second earring.

Roses for Elizabeth Bracelet

MATERIALS

BRACELET

5 floral lampwork beads (Lisa Kan Designs)

4 8mm faceted pink zirconia rounds

8 6mm mother-of-pearl rounds

10 4mm Crystal AB2x Swarovski bicones

2 2.5mm × 4mm sterling silver spacer beads

8 7mm sterling silver flower bead caps

1 sterling silver rose charm (Green Girl Studios)

11" (28cm) strand of .019" (.48mm) 49-strand wire

1 rose toggle clasp (Carl Clasmeyer)

1 8mm sterling silver jump ring

2 sterling silver crimp tubes

EARRING VARIATION

2 floral lampwork beads (Lisa Kan Designs)

4 8mm faceted pink zirconia rounds

2 6mm mother-of-pearl rounds

4 4mm Crystal AB2x Swarovski bicones

2 6mm × 9mm Swarovski Crystal teardrops

6 2.5mm × 4mm sterling silver spacer beads

4 7mm sterling silver flower bead caps

12" (30cm) piece of sterling silver chain

2 sterling silver shepherd's-hook ear wires

6 24-gauge sterling silver head pins

TOOLS

round-nose pliers

chain-nose pliers

bent-nose pliers or second pair of chain-nose pliers

flush cutters

flush cutters for beading wire

Elizabeth is my best friend. She writes incredible books on autism. One of her books was awarded the Autism Society of America's Literary Work of the Year, and she also received their Outstanding Parent Achievement Award. She is a very remarkable person, and I am proud to know her. I made this bracelet with Elizabeth and her love of roses in mind. I played up the soft ivory of the roses on the beads by using mother-of-pearl, and the pink is brought out with the pink zirconia rounds. A rose toggle added to a rose charm creates an effect that is extremely feminine and lacy. Whether you love roses, as Elizabeth does, or just love all things bright and beautiful, you are sure to enjoy this bracelet!

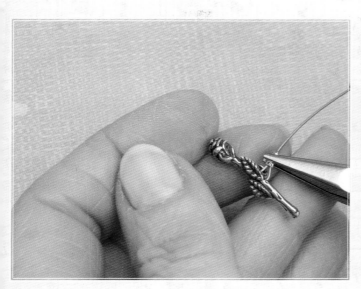

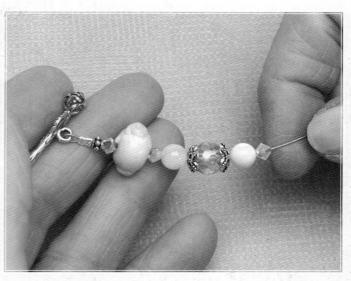

1. Crimp wire to clasp
Attach the 49-strand wire to the toggle clasp with a crimp tube (see Techniques, page 19).

2. String bracelet
Slide a spacer bead onto the wire. Add beads in the following pattern: Crystal AB2x bicone, lampwork bead, Crystal AB2x bicone, mother-of-pearl round, flower bead cap facing away from the mother-of-pearl, pink zirconia round, flower bead cap facing toward the pink zirconia, mother-of-pearl. Repeat the beading sequence four more times. End with a sterling spacer bead.

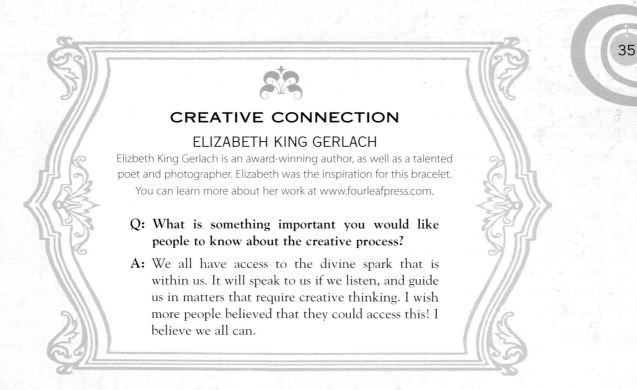

CREATIVE CONNECTION

ELIZABETH KING GERLACH

Elizbeth King Gerlach is an award-winning author, as well as a talented poet and photographer. Elizabeth was the inspiration for this bracelet. You can learn more about her work at www.fourleafpress.com.

Q: What is something important you would like people to know about the creative process?

A: We all have access to the divine spark that is within us. It will speak to us if we listen, and guide us in matters that require creative thinking. I wish more people believed that they could access this! I believe we all can.

3. Crimp bracelet closed
Attach the second piece of the toggle clasp to the free end of the wire strand with a crimp tube.

4. Add rose charm
Link the rose charm to the round piece of the toggle clasp with a jump ring.

ROSES FOR ELIZABETH EARRINGS

For each earring, cut a 2-link section of chain, a 5-link section of chain and a 7-link section of chain. Place the following beads on a head pin and link to the 2-link piece with a wire wrap: a Crystal AB2x bicone, a lampwork bead, a Crystal AB2x bicone and a spacer bead (see Techniques, pages 16–17). Place the following beads on a head pin and link to the 5-link piece of chain with a wire wrap: a pink zirconia round, a flower bead cap facing the pink zirconia, a mother-of-pearl round, a flower bead cap facing away from the mother-of-pearl, a pink zirconia round and a spacer bead. Place the following beads on a head pin and link to the 7-link piece of chain with a wire wrap: a Crystal teardrop and spacer bead. Open the loop at the bottom of the ear wire, hook the chain pieces onto the loop and close the ear wire. The dangles should hang shortest to longest, from the front of the earring.

CREATIVE CHALLENGE

Go to a garden nursery during the planting season and look at all the trees, bushes and flowers. Smell all the fragrances as they mix together in the warm breezes. Look at the colors around you and notice how they go together. Choose beads in the colors that strike you most and use them to create your own flower-inspired bracelet.

Treasured Friends Necklace

MATERIALS

15 6mm Aquamarine Swarovski rounds

12 sterling silver message beads (Nina Designs)

1 large sterling silver flower pendant (Nina Designs)

1 sterling silver adjustable hook-and-eye clasp (Nina Designs)

15 22-gauge decorative head pins (Nina Designs)

168 18-gauge, 5mm ID sterling silver jump rings (Urban Maille)

108 18-gauge, 4mm ID sterling silver jump rings (Urban Maille)

11 8mm sterling silver jump rings

16 6mm sterling silver jump rings

TOOLS

round-nose pliers

chain-nose pliers

bent-nose pliers or second pair of chain-nose pliers

flush cutters

∽ *TIP* ∽

The flower chain maille pattern used as the base of this necklace adds a very special touch when you use it in a complicated piece of jewelry, such as this necklace, but it is also very elegant unadorned.

I get excited just thinking about my bead friends! They possess so many amazing qualities, and I was able to express many of them in this necklace with message beads: vision, wisdom, joy, love, grace, friend, rebel, laugh, spirit, dream, hope and truth. The most important word I included to describe my friends is grace. However you interpret the word grace, it defines that something special in my friends. I placed these word beads on the necklace in pairs because what is one friend without another? I used a flower in full bloom as the centerpiece because my friends are so blooming *fabulous*! I included clear blue crystals because blue is such a serene color and beading gives my friends and me serenity. This chain maille necklace is my gift to them. I designed it to look like a treasure because I treasure them.

1. Create flower chain

Create fifty-five 3-ring flowers from the 5mm ID jump rings (see Techniques, page 15). To begin the flower chain, hook a 4mm ID jump ring through two flowers and close. Hook a second open jump ring through the two flowers, following the same path as the first, and close (see Techniques, page 14). Place a flower on an open jump ring, hook it to one of the flowers in the chain, and close the jump ring. Hook a second open ring along the same path as the first and close it. Continue until all the flowers are attached in a chain.

2. Attach clasp

Attach the clasp to the chain with one 8mm jump ring at each end.

3. Attach jump rings for dangles

Find the center flower of the chain and connect two 6mm jump rings to it. Working from the center outward, connect two 6mm jump rings to every fifth flower, repeating three times on both sides of the center flower. Attach all of the 6mm jump rings to the same side of the chain so the dangles will hang correctly.

4. Attach message bead dangles

To create the message bead dangles, slide a message bead and an Aquamarine round onto a decorative head pin and wire wrap it shut (see Techniques, pages 16–17). Use an 8mm jump ring to link two message bead dangles to each of the three pairs of 6mm jump rings on both sides of the center flower.

5. Attach pendant

Use an 8mm jump ring to link the flower pendant to the 6mm jump rings attached to the center flower of the chain.

6. Attach dangle to pendant

Slide an Aquamarine round onto a decorative head pin and wire wrap it closed. Repeat twice. Make one 3-ring flower from the remaining 5mm ID jump rings. Connect four 6mm jump rings to the flower unit. Place the Aquamarine dangles on an 8mm jump ring, hook it through two of the 6mm jump rings on the flower unit and close. Use an 8mm jump ring to connect the two free 6mm jump rings on the flower unit to the bottom loop on the back of the pendant.

Nancy's Dancing Pearls Bracelet

MATERIALS

60 4mm × 6mm top-drilled champagne pearls

6 4mm gold-filled rounds

8 4mm bright vermeil daisy spacers

16 5mm bright sterling silver daisy spacers

2 15" (38cm) strands of .019" (.48mm) 49-strand wire

1 flowered sterling silver box clasp (Nina Designs)

4 sterling silver crimp tubes

TOOLS

chain-nose pliers

flush cutters for beading wire

I t took us a long time to find a suitable school for my son Dylan, who has autism. We finally found a great place where the teachers are amazing. This year he has Bridget, Nancy and Donovan, his one-to-one aide. They are calming and kind. His teacher, Nancy, got the ball rolling for me to have jewelry shows at the school and also designed her own bracelet. This is Nancy's bracelet: a jubilant celebration of prettiness, motion and style, created with dancing, top-drilled pearls, and a gorgeous box clasp. It should be worn with a bounce in your step. I name this bracelet for a walking miracle: Dylan's wonderful teacher Nancy, who represents all of the teachers who walk with spirit and grace throughout my two autistic sons' school lives.

TIP

If made as instructed, this bracelet will measure 6¾" (17cm) long, which is a snug fit for the average wrist. The bracelet is snug so you can keep the clasp on top of your wrist to show it off. If you wish to lengthen or shorten the bracelet for comfort, add or subtract beads from each strand while maintaining the beading pattern.

1. Crimp first strand to clasp

Attach one piece of 49-strand wire to the box clasp with a crimp tube (see Techniques, page 19). Slide a silver daisy spacer, a vermeil daisy spacer and a silver daisy spacer over both ends of the wire.

2. String first strand of beads

String beads onto the wire in the following pattern: five pearls, gold-filled round, five more pearls, silver daisy spacer, vermeil daisy spacer, silver daisy spacer. Repeat this pattern two more times.

3. Crimp first strand closed

Attach the free end of the wire to the box clasp with a crimp tube.

4. String and wrap second strand

Attach the second 49-strand wire to the box clasp with a crimp tube. String the second strand exactly as the first strand. Wrap the second strand of the bracelet around the first strand four times. To finish, attach the second strand to the box clasp with a crimp tube.

NATURE

The Earth affects us every day in all kinds of ways. We can't help but be receptive to the amazing planet we live on. The elements are written about, tested, analyzed lyrically and scientifically, and yet we never lose our attraction to our environment.

From the viewpoint of a jewelry designer who often works with stones, wood and shells, it is doubly fascinating to me to explore what is going on in nature all the time. I am constantly searching out ways to use natural materials in my jewelry designs, such as in the Spice Market Earrings (page 66) and Citrus Gumdrop Necklace (page 56). Our beautiful world's influence upon my designs is undeniable. How can any of us shy away from where we breathe, eat and exist?

My memories are filled with natural beauty, and I draw from the world around me as I design jewelry. I spent my childhood vacations skin diving with my family in the Florida Keys and visiting the Adirondacks in upstate New York. I remember so much natural beauty in the places we visited. I also remember the natural beauty I found around my home. I made snow igloos as a little girl in my backyard when we had enough snow. If we didn't have enough snow, I made snow horses to ride on. And in the summer, my family went to the beach every day. Covered in suntan lotion, I opened myself up to the ceaseless wind and let it swoosh over me in currents. The waves of the Atlantic Ocean rushed over me endlessly as well. I walked carefully along the jetties, the pyrite in the jetty rocks winking and sparkling at me. My memories of the ocean inspired me to create the Trinity Spiral Necklace (page 64). I draw from all of these early influences when I design, as well as from the beauty surrounding me today. Go exploring in your natural world and find the things that inspire you!

In this chapter I will show off the world in all her brilliance to inspire you. Look around with your eyes wide open and see the beauty and wonder we are surrounded by every day.

Petals and Vines Bracelet and Earrings

MATERIALS

PETALS BRACELET

48 12mm × 30mm black ebony petal beads (The Bead Shop)

36 3.5mm sterling silver hex beads (The Bead Shop)

19 6mm Smokey Topaz Swarovski rounds

6 to 7 coils of stainless steel memory wire, bracelet size

2 26-gauge sterling silver head pins

2 6mm sterling silver jump rings

VINES EARRINGS

2 6mm Smokey Topaz Swarovski rounds

2 3.5mm sterling silver hex beads (The Bead Shop)

2 shibuichi "Seek Wisdom" links (Green Girl Studios)

2 sterling silver ear wires with ball tip

2 26-gauge sterling silver head pins

TOOLS

round-nose pliers

round-nose pliers for memory wire

chain-nose pliers

bent-nose pliers or second pair of chain-nose pliers

flush cutters

flush cutters for memory wire

The smooth texture of these ebony beads makes each piece feel like a touchstone; stringing this bracelet put me into a meditative mood. The look of the petals as they curl up your wrist is very organic. They have a graceful, natural flow. I chose to break up the stringing pattern as simply as possible, adding crystal rounds and sterling hex beads, so the ebony petals could shine. I wanted a special and unusual addition to this bracelet, so I created a pair of earrings using vine-patterned shibuichi components to reflect the curl of the ebony petals as they embrace your wrist. Shibuichi is a beautiful material composed of four parts copper and one part sterling silver. Different treatments can be used to produce a variety of colors of shibuichi. These links are the traditional color of shibuichi—red-orange—and they complement the other elements in this design. I further united the mood of the two pieces by using identical dangles at the ends of the earrings and bracelet.

TIP

My usual unspoken motto is, "The more the better!" However, sometimes less is more. If you come across something beautiful, like these ebony petals, let it shine by keeping the design simple.

PETALS BRACELET

1. Prepare memory wire

Make a neat loop at one end of the memory wire using round-nose pliers specifically meant for memory wire.

2. String beads

String beads onto the wire in the following pattern: hex bead, Smokey Topaz round, hex bead, three ebony petals. Repeat the pattern sixteen times, ending with a hex bead, Smokey Topaz round and hex bead.

3. Close bracelet

Push all of the beads together snugly. Cut the memory wire, leaving an end long enough to make another small loop. Loop the end of the memory wire using round-nose pliers specifically meant for memory wire.

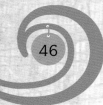

4. Attach dangle

Slide a Smokey Topaz round and a sterling hex bead onto a head pin and wire wrap the dangle closed (see Techniques, pages 16-17). Link this dangle to a memory wire loop with a jump ring. Repeat on the other side of the bracelet.

VINES EARRINGS

Slide a Smokey Topaz round and a sterling hex bead onto a head pin and wire wrap the dangle to a "Seek Wisdom" link (see Techniques, pages 16–17). To finish the earring, open the loop on the ear wire and slide the "Seek Wisdom" link onto the ear wire, making sure the vine side of the link is facing forward. Close the ear wire loop. Repeat for the second earring.

Earrings from the front

Earrings from the back

47

Portrait of Nature Necklace

MATERIALS

12 7mm-8mm sunstone rondelles

13 5mm-7mm baltic amber nuggets

1 sterling silver framed picture jasper pendant (The Bead Shop)

25" (64cm) length of sterling silver hammered decorative chain

36" (91cm) piece of 20-gauge dead soft sterling silver wire

1 vintage German glass clasp (Sojourner)

2 8mm sterling silver jump rings

TOOLS

round-nose pliers

chain-nose pliers

bent-nose pliers or second pair of chain-nose pliers

flush cutters

I cannot believe that a piece of picture jasper is anything but a real painting when I examine it. It looks like someone painted a tree on the stone in this pendant. Well, somebody did. Nature! To complement this beautiful pendant, I chose amber beads. I like having two types of natural stone in this piece. However, I then chose goldstone, a man-made stone composed of glass and copper. It complements the other elements because of its color, but it is also a contrast because it is man-made. To complete the design, I selected an interesting hammered chain with unexpected placement of the large ovals, small circles and connecting rings. To free up this design, I cut up the chain arbitrarily and randomly placed beads on each wire wrap. You can follow my design for your own creation, or randomly assemble your own.

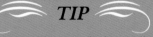

TIP

Be mindful of how your findings will affect your design, because findings add a lot to a design when you view it as a whole. Make sure to decide when you do (or don't) want the findings to have a major role in the appearance of a piece, and choose them accordingly.

1. Attach clasp

Attach one piece of the clasp to the chain by hooking a jump ring through the loop on the clasp and a small connector ring on an oval link of the chain.

2. Build chain

Count off a large oval link, a small round link, a large oval link, a small round link, a large oval link and a small round link. Cut the chain, leaving the small connector ring on the last round link. All wire wraps will link to these connector rings, so do not cut them off! Wrap a 7" (18cm) piece of wire to the small connector ring and string two amber nuggets and two sunstone rondelles onto the wire (see Techniques, page 17). Wrap the free end of the wire to a small connector ring attached to a small round link on the chain.

3. Add pendant

Count off a small round link and a large oval link and cut the chain, leaving the small connector ring attached. Wrap a 7" (18cm) piece of wire to the small connector ring and string a sunstone rondelle and three amber nuggets onto the wire. Wrap the free end of the wire to the chain at a small connector ring attached to a large oval link. Count off a large oval link and two small round links. Cut the chain, leaving the small connector ring. Wrap an 8" (20cm) piece of wire to the small connector ring and string two sunstone rondelles and three amber nuggets onto the wire. Slide the pendant onto the wire and position it so the bail of the pendant sits on the amber nuggets. Slide two more sunstone rondelles onto the wire.

4. Finish chain

Wrap the free end of the wire to the chain at a small connector ring attached to a small round link. Gently bend the wire the pendant is on into a slight curve. Count off a small round link, a large oval link and a small round link and cut the chain, leaving a connector ring. Wrap a 7" (18cm) piece of wire to the connector ring and string two amber nuggets and three sunstone rondelles onto the wire. Wrap the free end of the wire to the chain at a small connector ring attached to a small round link. Count off a small round link, a large oval link, a small round link and a large oval link and cut the chain, leaving the small connector ring. Wrap a 7" (18cm) piece of wire to the small connector ring and string a sunstone rondelle, two amber nuggets, a sunstone rondelle and an amber nugget on the wire. Wrap the free end of the wire to the chain at a small connector ring attached to a large oval link. Count off a large oval link, a small round link, a large oval link, a small round link and a large oval link. Cut the chain, leaving a small connector ring. To finish, attach the second half of the clasp to the last connector ring with a jump ring.

Magnificent Mineral Lariat

MATERIALS

LARIAT

4 7mm–7.5mm white freshwater pearls

3 11mm tourmilated quartz faceted coins

1 10mm × 19mm green Phantom crystal faceted triangle tube

4 3mm–4mm faceted smokey quartz rondelles

4 8mm sterling silver hammered dome bead caps (The Bead Shop)

6 20mm × 29mm sterling silver coin-style pendants (The Bead Shop)

1 14mm sterling silver hammered ring

3 39" (99cm) lengths of figure-eight sterling silver chain

8 24-gauge sterling silver head pins

13 6mm sterling silver jump rings

EARRING VARIATION

2 7mm–7.5mm white freshwater pearls

2 3mm–4mm faceted smokey quartz rondelles

2 8mm sterling silver hammered dome bead caps

2 20mm × 29mm sterling silver coin-style pendants

2 sterling silver ear wires

2 24-gauge sterling silver head pins

TOOLS

round-nose pliers

chain-nose pliers

bent-nose pliers or second pair of chain-nose pliers

flush cutters

What glorious minerals Nature has created! The rutilated quartz beads, with their amazing striations, make me want to learn everything I can about stones. The Phantom crystal fascinates me. I chose the components for this lariat to suit each other well. The sterling Roman-style coins look antique, and the dome bead caps and hammered ring mirror this look. The pearls look outstanding in this rugged setting and really hold their own with the other charms. This lariat has a lot of punch and elemental strength to it, yet the delicate chain lightens the look. There are many ways to wear this lariat: Wear it to the side, take it from front to back and around again like a double necklace, or loop it around and just tie it. I even made my lariat extra long so I could use it as a belt. You can be just as creative about wearing this lariat as you are when designing it!

1. Connect chains

Hook all three chains onto a single jump ring to connect them. Repeat on the other end, being careful not to twist or tangle the chains.

2. Prepare dangles

Slide a pearl, a bead cap and a smokey quartz rondelle onto a head pin and wire wrap the dangle closed (see Techniques, pages 16–17). Repeat three times. Place a tourmilated quartz coin on a head pin and wire wrap it closed. Make two more quartz dangles. Place the Phantom crystal on a head pin and wire wrap it closed. Working from left to right, connect the following dangles to the hammered ring with jump rings: The Phantom crystal dangle, a coin-style pendant, a pearl dangle and a quartz coin dangle. Working from left to right, connect the following dangles with a jump ring: a quartz coin dangle on a jump ring, a coin-style pendant on a jump ring, a quartz coin dangle on a jump ring and three pearl dangles on a single jump ring. Place a coin-style pendant on a jump ring. Repeat twice. Link two of the coin-style pendants together for a 2-coin unit.

3. Attach dangles to one side

Open one of the jump rings connecting the chains. Slide the 2-coin unit and the silver hammered ring onto the jump ring and close.

4. Attach dangles to other side

Open the jump ring on the other end of the chains. Slide a coin-style pendant on a jump ring, a coin-style pendant and the linked dangles onto the jump ring and close it.

MAGNIFICENT MINERAL EARRINGS

Slide a pearl, a bead cap and a smokey quartz rondelle onto a head pin and wire wrap the dangle closed. Open the ear wire, place a coin pendant and the pearl dangle onto the ear wire and close it. Repeat for the second earring.

Turning Leaf Earrings

52

I love these champagne side-drilled cubic zirconia pear beads. I just had to use them in this pretty design! That meant I would be wire wrapping them from the side in order to attach them to the leaf components. I hated doing this type of wire wrap for years. However, these beautiful beads forced me to learn the right way to do it. The Copper Swarovski bicones and the Vintage Rose Swarovski bicones are sweet color choices with the champagne pear beads. I particularly like the way the rose gold-filled balls complement the autumnal, leafy colors. The copper balls on the sterling ear wires and the brass jump rings are perfect for the color mix as well. These earrings don't use natural materials, but they are inspired by Nature and her gorgeous fall trees.

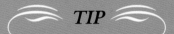

TIP

If you like green, this design is fun for a fresh spring look. Simply select beads in tones of green. Or, consider silver findings and plain Crystal Swarovski bicones with pretty white drop pearls for a wintertime look. The leaf chandelier components are a fantastic and flexible jumping-off point for so many great creations. Start by thinking about the beautiful, changing colors of all the seasons.

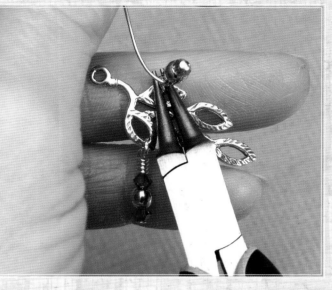

1. Attach top dangles

Slide a Crystal Copper bicone, a rose gold-filled round and a Crystal Copper bicone onto a head pin. Wire wrap the dangle to the top left leaf on the chandelier (see Techniques, pages 16–17). Repeat on the top right leaf.

2. Begin pear dangles

Slide a cubic zirconia pear bead to the middle of a 3½" (9cm) piece of wire. Cross the wires. Bend the wire that is now on the right side of the bead to a 90° angle.

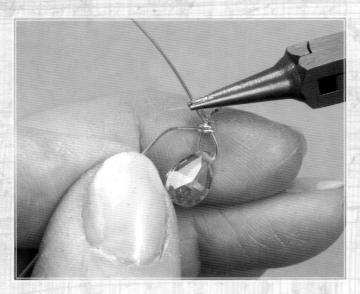

3. Begin coil

Create a loop in the bent wire as if you were creating a wire wrap. Begin coiling the wire used to make the loop around both the base of the loop and the second piece of wire.

4. Trim ends

Cut the end of the coiled wire and flatten the cut tip into the coil. Cut the end of the wire that is sticking out of the top of the coil. Repeat Steps 2–4 and wrap each pear bead.

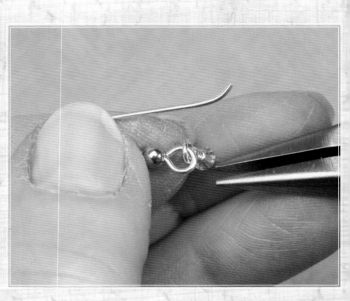

5. Attach pear dangles

Attach one pear dangle to each of the three bottom leaves on the chandelier finding with a brass jump ring.

6. Attach dangle to ear wire

Slide a Vintage Rose bicone onto a head pin and wire wrap it to the loop of the ear wire.

7. Finish earring

Open the ear wire and attach the chandelier dangle behind the Vintage Rose dangle. Close the ear wire. Repeat Steps 1–7 for the second earring.

CREATIVE CHALLENGE

Examine a book of beautiful photography. Don't just try to find inspiration from obvious sources, like fashion and jewelry. Look at photography books about nature, architecture or any other subject that interests you. Study the play of light, color and space. Use the elements that appeal to you, such as colors and shapes, in your next design.

Citrus Gumdrop Necklace

MATERIALS

NECKLACE

8 12mm butterscotch resin dice
(Artbeads.com)

13 12mm pumpkin resin dice
(Artbeads.com)

18 3mm sterling silver seamless beads

7 8mm × 18mm porcelain tube beads
(Artbeads.com)

1 20mm × 30mm natural wood frame
(Artbeads.com)

30" (76cm) piece of .019" (.48mm) 49-
strand wire

1 small sterling silver lobster claw clasp

1 22-gauge sterling silver head pin

2 7mm sterling silver soldered jump rings

4 sterling silver crimp tubes

EARRING VARIATION

2 12mm pumpkin resin dice

2 3mm sterling silver seamless beads

2 8mm × 18mm porcelain tube beads

2 20mm × 30mm natural wood frame

2 6mm sterling silver and citrine
earring posts

2 22-gauge sterling silver head pins

TOOLS

round-nose pliers

chain-nose pliers

bent-nose pliers (optional)

flush cutters

flush cutters for beading wire

This necklace shows how wood combined with man-made components creates a harmonious design when shape, balance, color and placement are all taken into account. I kicked off the design with a fascinating carved wooden frame. The shape of the colorful resin dice complements the wooden frame, while the porcelain tubes coordinate with both the resin and the wood, drawing the design together. These elements create a necklace that is contemporary, fun to wear and chic. Plus, the resin cubes resemble those chewy movie theater candies. Did I feel like eating them as I made this? You bet I did!

TIP

Experiment with different colors for the resin and porcelain beads. Many colors will look great with these wood frames. Larger silver rounds will also change the look of this necklace by creating more space in the design.

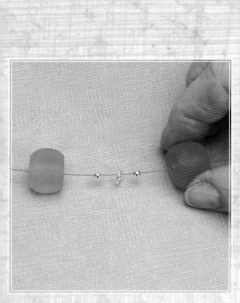

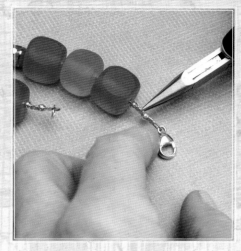

1. Begin stringing beads

Place a soldered jump ring on the 49-strand wire. On either side of the jump ring, string a silver bead and a butterscotch die.

2. Continue stringing

Continue stringing beads in the following pattern on either side of the center: a porcelain bead, a pumpkin die, a silver bead, a butterscotch die, a silver bead, a pumpkin die. Repeat this pattern a total of three times on each side of the necklace.

3. Attach clasp

Attach the lobster claw clasp to one end of the necklace with a beaded double crimp using a silver bead (see Techniques, page 19). Attach a soldered jump ring to the other end of the necklace with a beaded double crimp.

4. Attach pendant

Place a porcelain bead inside the wood frame and slide a head pin through the holes in both. Place a pumpkin die and a silver bead on top of the wood frame on the head pin. Wire wrap the pendant to the soldered jump ring at the center of the necklace (see Techniques, pages 16–17).

CITRUS GUMDROP EARRINGS

Place a porcelain tube bead inside a wood frame and slip the beads onto a head pin. Place a pumpkin die and a silver bead on top of the wood frame on the head pin. Wire wrap the beaded head pin to the citrine earring post (see Techniques, pages 16–17). Repeat for the other earring.

Spiral Earrings

MATERIALS

12 4mm garnet rounds

2 6mm burgundy Rococo Miyuki beads (Shepherdess Beads)

20" (51cm) piece of 16-gauge dead soft sterling silver wire

8" (20cm) piece of 18-gauge dead soft sterling silver wire

2 sterling silver ear wires with silver bead

12 26-gauge sterling silver beaded head pins

TOOLS

round-nose pliers

chain-nose pliers

flat-nose pliers

bent-nose pliers or second pair of chain-nose pliers

flush cutters

TIP

There are many colors of garnet. In fact, you can obtain garnet in every color except blue. Try Hessonite garnet, with its rich orangey-yellow tones, Rhodolite garnet, a gorgeous pinky purple, or Tsavorite garnet, a lovely, ritzy green.

I wanted to convey a Victorian feeling with these earrings. The Victorians loved garnet and used it often in their jewelry. Garnets are found in lots of places, and apparently Long Island, New York, is one of them. I remember my mother digging around in our front yard one year, separating lily of the valley so it would have more room to spread and grow. One day, she happened to dig up a plain-looking rock while she was working. She went off for a second and returned with a hammer. She gave the rock a few sharp cracks and it split open revealing a hidden treasure: garnets! What an amazing sight it was for me! Who knew I had gemstones buried in my yard? Apparently my mother did.

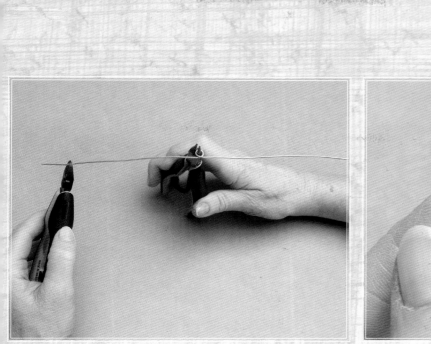

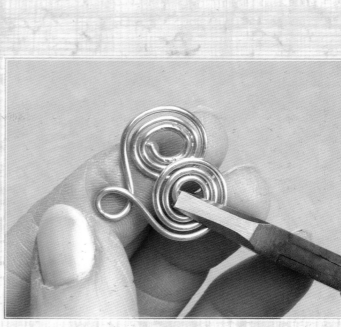

1. Loop wire

Begin by cutting the 16-gauge wire into two 10" (25cm) pieces. Straighten and work-harden a piece of wire with wire straighteners or by running a cloth along it. Pinch the midpoint of the wire with round-nose pliers and smoothly pull the ends of the wire around the pliers to form a loop. Trim the wire so it is the same length on both sides of the loop.

2. Spiral wire

Use round-nose pliers to make a loop at one end of the wire. Switch to flat-nose pliers and make a tight spiral toward the middle of the wire. Repeat with the other end. The two spirals will overlap slightly.

59

3. Attach garnet dangles

Slide a garnet round onto a beaded head pin and attach to the bottom of the left wire spiral with a bundled wire wrap (see Techniques, page 18). Repeat twice more on the left spiral and three times on the right. You may have to spread out the wire spiral a bit in order to get the dangles to hang properly.

4. Wire wrap Miyuki bead

Wrap a 4" (10cm) piece of 18-gauge wire to the top loop in the wire (see Techniques, page 17). Slide a Rococo Miyuki bead onto the wire and close it with a wire wrap.

5. Attach ear wire

Open the ear wire and hook onto the Miyuki wire wrap. Close the ear wire. Repeat Steps 1–5 for the second earring.

Delicate Necklace

MATERIALS

NECKLACE

168 3.5mm faceted multicolor sapphires

1 12mm × 8mm × 3mm sterling silver feather charm (Nina Designs)

19½" (50cm) segment of 5mm sterling silver chain

1 sterling silver hook-and-eye feather clasp (Nina Designs)

28 26-gauge sterling silver beaded head pins

2 6mm sterling silver jump rings

2 4mm sterling silver jump rings

EARRING VARIATION

12 3.5mm multicolor faceted sapphires

2 small sterling silver ear wires with silver bead

2 26-gauge sterling silver beaded head pins

TOOLS

round-nose pliers

chain-nose pliers

bent-nose pliers or second pair of chain-nose pliers

flush cutters

A beautiful song, "Delicate" by Damien Rice, compelled me to create this elegant, earthy, yet very feminine necklace. Because I had the word "delicate" running through my head, I wanted everything in this design to reflect that word. I chose tiny, multicolored, faceted sapphires and placed the different colors randomly in the design, the way nature seems to choose her colors. I suspended these gorgeous gems from a handmade silver chain, and they move to and fro in a sweet manner. The pendant and matching clasp are small and quite simple. They have a lovely pressed-leaf pattern, as if they were gathered up from some primordial place. This is appropriate to the feeling of the song. I love this beautiful necklace. That is what you achieve when you use a favorite song to pull up some inspiration in your design.

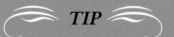

TIP

An easy way to find the center of a piece of chain is to place a piece of wire through a link in the chain and let the chain hang down from the wire. When the two ends of the chain hang down evenly, you have found the center link.

1. Attach pendant

Place the feather charm on a 4mm jump ring. Hook a second 4mm jump ring through the first jump ring and through the center link of the chain. Close the jump ring.

2. Attach dangles

Slide six sapphire beads onto a head pin. Count two links to the left of the feather charm and wire wrap the beaded dangle to the chain (see Techniques, pages 16–17). Repeat thirteen more times on the left of the charm, wire wrapping sapphire dangles every two links. Repeat fourteen times to the right of the feather charm. Wrap all of the head pins to the same side of the chain so the dangles hang correctly.

3. Attach clasp

Link the clasp to the ends of the chain with 6mm jump rings.

DELICATE EARRINGS

Slide six sapphire beads onto a head pin and wire wrap the head pin closed (see Techniques, pages 16–17). Open the ear wire, place the dangle on the ear wire and close it. Repeat for the second earring.

61

"It's not that we're scared/
It's just that it's delicate."—Damien Rice

With thanks to Damien Rice: song by Damien Rice
(www.DamienRice.com), publishing administered by Warner Chappell.

Blooming Chain Maille Earrings

MATERIALS

2 pressed-flower dangles (Fusion Beads)

2 lever-back sterling silver ear wires

36 18-gauge, 6mm ID sterling silver jump rings (Urban Maille)

22 18-gauge, 3.25mm ID sterling silver jump rings (Urban Maille)

TOOLS

chain-nose pliers

bent-nose pliers or second pair of chain-nose pliers

CREATIVE CONNECTION

AISLYN

Aislyn is a talented chain maille artist as well as co-owner of Urban Maille (www.urbanmaille.com).

Q: What would you like people to know about the creative process?

A: There will always be obstacles to anything you want to do, but focusing on the obstacles only drives you into them…. If you focus on the obstacles, on all the reasons why not, you will simply hit one obstacle after another. If you see the obstacle but focus on picking a path around it, then the obstacle doesn't stop you. It might change your path a little, it might add a bit of time to your trip, but it doesn't stop you from getting where you want to go.

It's so alluring to have a bit of color accenting your face. The minute I saw these enchanting pressed-flower pendants, I knew they would be perfect components in an earring design. I love the way the flowers curl as though they are frozen in time, still growing just the way they were when first picked. I used a simple chain maille design to punctuate the prettiness of the pressed flowers, and I balanced the size of the chain maille with the flower dangle. What could be a better way to show off your skills as a jewelry maker than flowers with chain maille?

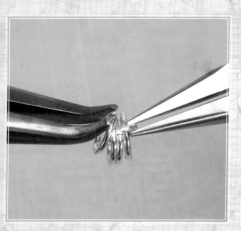

1. Start captured chain

Place four 6mm ID jump rings on a 3.25mm ID jump ring and close it. Attach a second 3.25mm ID jump ring next to the first (see Techniques, page 14).

2. Add interior ring

Open a 6mm ID jump ring and hook it around both 3.25mm ID jump rings and between the 6mm ID jump rings so that two 6mm ID jump rings rest on either side of the newly added ring, as shown. Close the newly added 6mm ID jump ring. The newly added ring does not go through any rings. It should be parallel to the 6mm ID jump rings and perpendicular to the 3.25mm ID jump rings.

3. Continue building captured chain

Flip one 6mm ID jump ring up on each side of the 3.25mm ID rings so that the ring wrapped around the 3.25mm ID jump rings is sandwiched by two 6mm jump rings on each side of the 3.25mm ID jump rings. Hook a 3.25mm ID jump ring through the two upright rings. Add a 6mm ID jump ring to each side of the open 3.25mm ID jump ring. Close the 3.25mm ID jump ring. Attach a second 3.25mm ID jump ring, following the path of the first. Again, wrap a 6mm ID jump ring around the 3.25mm ID jump rings and between the 6mm ID jump rings. Continue adding rings in this pattern until there are five pairs of 3.25mm ID jump rings.

4. Join chain into a circle

Coil the chain into a circle and connect the two ends with two 3.25mm ID jump rings, forming a circle of chain maille.

5. Attach flower dangle

Place a flower dangle on a 6mm ID jump ring. Attach the dangle to the chain maille circle at the two 6mm ID jump rings opposite the 3.25mm ID jump rings used to connect the circle. Attach a second 6mm ID jump ring parallel to the first.

6. Attach ear wire

Wrap a 6mm ID jump ring around the 3.25mm ID jump rings used to connect the circle and close the jump ring. Attach a second 6mm ID jump ring following the same path. Hook the ear wire onto a 3.25mm ID jump ring and attach it to the two 6mm ID jump rings. Repeat Steps 1–6 for the second earring.

Trinity Spiral Necklace

64

MATERIALS

NECKLACE

280 3mm-4mm heishi shell disk beads (enough to string 10½" [27cm])

1 round focal shell bead (Artbeads.com)

44 3mm seamless sterling silver beads

29" (74cm) strand of .019" (.48mm) 49-strand wire

1 sterling silver S-clasp

2 6mm soldered sterling silver jump rings

4 sterling silver crimp tubes

EARRING VARIATION

60 heishi shell beads

28 3mm seamless sterling silver round beads

2 sterling silver 5-loop T-station chandelier components (Artbeads.com)

2 sterling silver ear wires

8 24-gauge sterling silver head pins

TOOLS

round-nose pliers

chain-nose pliers

bent-nose pliers or second pair of chain-nose pliers

flush cutters

flush cutters for beading wire

The carved shell focal bead featured in this necklace intrigued me. It is a cowrie shell carved with a trinity spiral design. It reminds me of waves curling in a never-ending current. With such a strong focal bead as the beginning of my design, I decided to keep the rest of the design simple. I chose green oyster heishi shell beads to continue the ocean theme of the necklace. I added sterling silver beads in groups of three, reflecting the trinity spiral in the focal bead. The sterling silver beads punctuate the design, breaking up the heishi shell beads and adding interest. I think this necklace shows that simple can be beautiful, and I hope you agree.

CREATIVE CHALLENGE

Find inspiration from a sense you probably don't associate with jewelry—your sense of smell. Scents can be very evocative. Find a scent that holds a strong memory for you and draw on that memory for fresh design ideas. Maybe the scent of the ocean would inspire you to create a beach-themed necklace like this one.

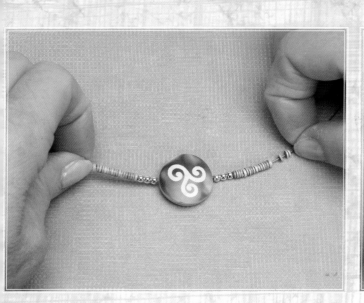

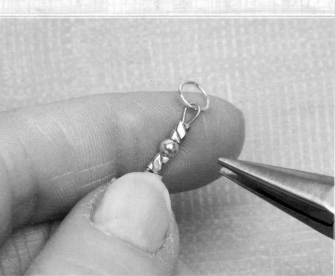

1. String beads

Slide the focal bead onto the 49-strand wire. String beads on both sides of the focal bead in the following pattern: three silver beads, ¾" (2cm) of heishi beads (approximately twenty beads). Repeat the beading pattern a total of seven times on both sides of the focal bead.

2. Crimp necklace closed

Use crimp tubes and silver beads to double crimp both sides of the necklace closed with a soldered jump ring at each end (see Techniques, page 19).

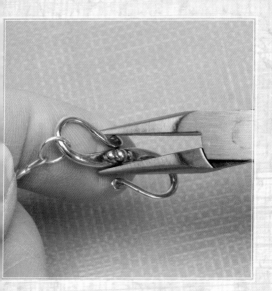

3. Attach S-clasp

Hook one side of the S-clasp through a soldered jump ring. Use chain-nose pliers to squeeze shut the end on the jump ring. Leave the other side of the S-clasp open so it can easily hook through the other jump ring to open and close the necklace.

TRINITY SPIRAL EARRINGS

Place five heishi beads and three silver beads on a head pin and wire wrap the dangle to the first loop on the T-station (see Techniques, pages 16–17). Repeat on the last loop on the T-station. Place three silver beads, ten heishi beads and one silver bead on a head pin and wrap to the second loop on the T-station. Repeat on the third loop on the T-station. Open the ear wire and place the T-station on it. Close the ear wire. Repeat for the second earring.

Spice Market Earrings

MATERIALS

SPICE MARKET EARRINGS

2 decorated lac beads (Bead 'n Shop)

8 5mm vermeil daisy spacers

4 vermeil hex beads (The Bead Shop)

2 gold-filled ear wires

2 24-gauge vermeil head pins

SPICE MARKET EARRING VARIATION

2 decorated lac beads (Bead 'n Shop)

4 3mm sterling silver stardust rounds

2 gold lever-back ear wires

2 24-gauge gold head pins with bezel-set diamonds (The Bead Shop)

TOOLS

round-nose pliers

chain-nose pliers

bent-nose pliers or second pair of chain-nose pliers

flush cutters

Created from the hardened resin of the *Kerria lacca* insect, lac is an incredible natural material. The resin has been tempered by human hands to bring out its loveliness. All you have to do to make a design with a lac bead is to take one look, and you will be in love. This is the start of endless possibilities if you use your imagination. Lac beads have their own built-in design inspirations—studying the decorations imbedded in the bead is a great way to start designing. The earrings I made are stacked with charming vermeil daisy spacers and I used vermeil ear wires to coordinate with the decorations in the lac bead I chose. The bead is what it's all about!

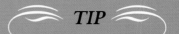

TIP

Feel free to dress these earrings up as much as you want! For the variation pair, I used head pins with diamonds on the ends. The sky (or maybe your budget) is the limit!

1. Place beads on head pin

Place a hex bead, two daisy spacers, a lac bead, two daisy spacers and a hex bead on a head pin.

2. Wire wrap head pin

Wire wrap the head pin closed (see Techniques, pages 16-17).

3. Attach ear wire

Open the ear wire and place the beaded head pin on it. Repeat Steps 1–3 for the second earring.

SPICE MARKET EARRING VARIATION

Place a stardust round, a lac bead and a stardust round on a diamond head pin. Wire wrap the head pin closed (see Techniques, pages 16–17). Open the ear wire and place the beaded head pin on it. Repeat for the second earring.

Fairy in the Garden Necklace

MATERIALS

42 large turquoise teardrop beads

18 3mm × 6mm rose quartz rondelles

18 crystal chip beads

1 turquoise lampwork vessel and matching round bead (Kim Miles)

1 shibuichi fairy centerpiece (Green Girl Studios)

2 20" (51cm) strands of .019" (.48mm) 49-strand wire

8" (20cm) piece of 20-gauge dead soft sterling silver wire

1 shibuichi heart-and-key toggle clasp (Green Girl Studios)

2 24-gauge sterling silver head pins

3 6mm natural brass jump rings

4 sterling silver crimp tubes

TOOLS

round-nose pliers

chain-nose pliers

bent-nose pliers or second pair of chain-nose pliers

flush cutters

flush cutters for beading wire

When I was small, I thought I would find a fairy or a magical creature just around the next corner. Now I am older, but I haven't lost the feeling that they are there, waiting. This necklace represents my fantasy childhood: lush, fanciful and bountiful. I wanted to use very natural-looking stones because I imagine fairies live in wild places. The turquoise was perfect for this, with its crackly black pattern, and the non-uniform cutting of the teardrops. I added crystal chips and rose quartz to unify the necklace with the rose color of the fairy centerpiece. Designing this necklace made me feel as though I had come upon a fairy's secret garden.

CREATIVE CONNECTION
KIM MILES

Kim Miles is an award-winning lampwork bead artist. The lampwork vessel used in this necklace is one of her creations. You can see more of her work at www.kimmiles.com.

Q: What would you like people to know about the creative process?

A: There was an art teacher in high school who told us, "Perfection is boring." I still love her for that. Even though I wandered away from art for years, remembering what she said gave me permission to take risks in life that wouldn't have been possible if perfection had been important to me.

1. Add dangles to centerpiece

Place a crystal chip bead and a rose quartz rondelle on a head pin and close the dangle with a bundled wire wrap (see Techniques, page 18). Attach the dangle to the bottom wing of the fairy centerpiece with a brass jump ring. Repeat on the other wing.

2. Attach bead wire

Use crimp tubes to crimp bead wire to both of the top wings of the fairy centerpiece (see Techniques, page 19).

3. String beads

String beads on both sides of the fairy centerpiece in the following pattern: rose quartz rondelle, crystal chip bead, three turquoise teardrop beads, crystal chip bead, rose quartz rondelle, three turquoise teardrop beads. Repeat the pattern three times on each side of the centerpiece, ending on a rose quartz rondelle, crystal chip bead, three turquoise teardrop beads, crystal chip bead, rose quartz rondelle.

4. Attach clasp

Crimp each end of the necklace closed, adding the heart-and-key toggle clasp.

5. Create vessel dangle

Wire wrap the silver wire to the handle of the lampwork vessel (see Techniques, page 17). Place the lampwork round on the wire and wire wrap it closed.

6. Attach vessel dangle

Attach the vessel dangle to the bottom of the fairy centerpiece with a brass jump ring.

Golden Hues Bracelet and Earrings

MATERIALS

GOLDEN HUES BRACELET

2 16mm × 30mm melo shell beads (The Bead Shop)

7 vermeil triangle beads

4 6mm Turquoise Swarovski rounds

6 vermeil hex beads (The Bead Shop)

15" (38cm) strand of .019" (.48mm) 49-strand wire

1 vermeil spiral toggle clasp

2 gold-filled crimp tubes

GOLDEN HUES EARRINGS

2 carved bone beads with stone inlay (The Bead Shop)

2 6mm Turquoise Swarovski rounds

4 vermeil hex beads (The Bead Shop)

2 gold-filled ear wires with gold-filled bead

2 24-gauge vermeil head pins with ball

TOOLS

round-nose pliers

chain-nose pliers

bent-nose pliers or second pair of chain-nose pliers

flush cutters

flush cutters for beading wire

I designed this bracelet and earring set to play off the great colors of these beautiful melo shell beads. I love their stunning orange, yellow and golden tones. The turquoise Swarovski rounds are a super counterpoint to the golden hues. Shell can be a great addition to casual jewelry; however, to create something more formal, I added elaborate triangle vermeil beads and a scrolled clasp. These accents give the bracelet a more polished look. The accompanying earrings may look like shell, but they are actually bone with inlaid designs. I used components from the bracelet in the earrings, such as the turquoise beads and the hex beads, to bring the two pieces together.

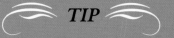

TIP

Don't be afraid to unite unique materials in unusual designs. If you think through the design and relate the pieces, it will end up looking terrific!

GOLDEN HUES BRACELET

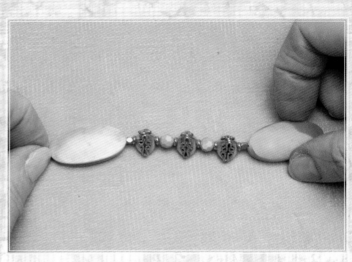

1. Begin stringing beads

Slide a triangle bead, a Turquoise round, a triangle bead, a Turquoise round and a triangle bead onto the 49-strand wire.

2. String shell beads

Slide a hex bead, a shell bead and a hex bead onto the 49-strand wire. Repeat on the other side of the wire.

3. Finish stringing beads

On both sides of the bracelet, add a triangle bead, a Turquoise round, a triangle bead and a hex bead.

4. Attach clasp

Crimp each end of the bracelet, adding the spiral toggle clasp (see Techniques, page 19).

GOLDEN HUES EARRINGS

Place a hex bead, a Turquoise round, a bone bead and a hex bead on a head pin and wire wrap the dangle closed (see Techniques, pages 16–17). Open an ear wire and place the bone dangle on the ear wire. To finish, close the ear wire. Repeat for the second earring.

Indian Summer Necklace

72

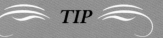

TIP

You need quite a bit of wrist power when working with such heavy-gauge jump rings. Take a break when your wrists are tired.

I started this design with a large, iridescent blacklip shell. It shimmers in a cool, moody way. I wire wrapped the shell so it lies under a hammered sterling disk. Together, they resemble the full moon on a night in early autumn. Add the glittering glass leaves and the drop crystals, and you can almost feel the moonlight streaming through the trees, throwing shadows over everything you see on a perfect Indian summer evening. Instead of using a single chain, I balanced the large pendant by adding double strands of jump rings in sections as I wove the chain. Let this necklace call you to come out and play in the night as the seasons change.

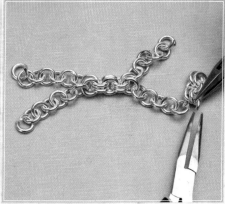

1. Make 2-ring units

Hook an open 5.5mm ID jump ring through two closed 5.5mm ID jump rings and close it. Link a second open jump ring through the two closed jump rings, following the same path as the first ring, and close it (see Techniques, page 14).

Hook an open jump ring through the two newly added rings and close it. Add another jump ring, following the same path as the first ring, and close it, creating a piece of chain with three 2-ring units.

Create eight more pieces of chain with three 2-ring units.

2. Build chain

Hook a jump ring through the last two rings of a chain unit and close. Hook a jump ring through the ring that was just added and close. Continue adding rings, one into the other, until seven rings have been added, forming a simple chain. Repeat once in the same 2-ring unit and twice in the 2-ring unit on the opposite end of the chain unit, creating an X when spread out.

Connect a new chain unit to the simple chains with jump rings as shown. Continue building the necklace by connecting chain units with simple chain. Finish with a chain unit at both ends.

3. Attach clasp

Slide the S-clasp through the last 2-ring unit on the chain. Use chain-nose pliers to close the end of the S-clasp attached to the chain. Leave the other side of the S-clasp open so it can easily hook through the other half of the chain to open and close the necklace.

4. Create shell dangle

Join the hammered silver disk to the shell pendant with a bundled wire wrap on the silver wire (see Techniques, page 18). Place three spacer beads on the wire and close it with a bundled wire wrap. Place the shell dangle on an 8mm jump ring.

5. Create leaf dangle

Use an 8mm jump ring to attach a glass leaf to the first link of the cable chain. Attach the remaining leaves to the chain every two links. Attach the leaves to the same side of the chain so they hang properly. Place a Light Colorado Topaz teardrop on a head pin and wire wrap closed (see Techniques, pages 16–17). Repeat with the remaining teardrop beads. Place two Topaz dangles and one Crystal dangle on an 8mm jump ring and attach to the last link in the chain. Place two Crystal dangles on a jump ring and attach this to the last link in the chain as well.

6. Attach dangles to chain

Place one Topaz dangle and one Crystal dangle on an 8mm jump ring and attach to the second-to-last link. Place two Topaz dangles and one Crystal dangle on an 8mm jump ring and attach to the link next to the last leaf. Hook an 8mm jump ring through the middle 2-ring unit of the jump ring chain. Place the shell dangle and the leaf dangle on the open jump ring and close it. The leaf dangle should hang to the front of the shell dangle.

73

BEAD BOX

This chapter is the freewheeling maverick of the book! We all have a bead box or two (or five hundred) holding beads that are waiting patiently to be rediscovered and used. Let your hidden treasure inspire you. There are plenty of times when I don't have an exact plan for what I want to design next. I view this as pure fun because I feel free to do anything! I can experiment and play when I open my bead box to see what I have, and I did just that when I created a Trio of Sparkling Earrings (page 110). Gather together a collection of interesting stones, beads, chain and leather. Try new shapes, new materials and new techniques. Start creating without any plan to guide you.

Many of the designs in this chapter appear as if I chose in advance what to do, when actually they grew organically from one single point, such as the Edward the Sheep Bracelet (page 96). I simply took materials and used them to their best advantage. Some projects come tripping off my fingers as if someone is standing behind me, telling me how to create the piece. Inspiration comes from any and every direction, sometimes taking me completely by surprise! This serendipity gives these pieces, such as the Art House Bracelet (page 104), a special charm and even a capricious quality.

When you design in this manner, you may not always have results you are happy with, but I recommend messing up on a regular basis. Those flawed pieces can be (with a little more work and refinement) stepping stones to a successful piece of jewelry. Dive in and see what is offered here. It is a fascinating journey when you use your bead box, coupled with your imagination and skills, to create some spectacular and one-of-a-kind pieces of jewelry!

Two Serendipitous Bracelets

MATERIALS

RUBY COIN BRACELET

2 16mm ruby zoisite coins

4 6mm Tanzanite Swarovski faceted spacer beads

2 8mm Kambaba jasper rondelles

1 11mm sterling silver daisy bead (Nina Designs)

1 ¾" (2cm) oval quartz bead

6 links of textured and smooth sterling silver cable chain

36" (91cm) piece of 20-gauge dead soft sterling silver wire

1 15mm sterling silver leaf toggle clasp (Fusion Beads)

3 22-gauge sterling silver head pins

RICE JASPER BRACELET

1 12mm × 36mm black-and-white jasper rice bead

2 rose quartz chips

3 8mm faceted clear cubic zirconia beads

6 5mm oxidized sterling silver daisy spacers

1 8mm oxidized sterling silver bead cap

5 links textured oxidized sterling silver chain

3" (8cm) piece of black braided leather

8" (20cm) piece of 20-gauge dead soft sterling silver wire

1 sterling silver figure-eight clasp

3 22-gauge sterling silver head pins

1 8mm sterling silver jump ring

2 6mm sterling silver crimps

TOOLS

round-nose pliers

chain-nose pliers

flat-nose pliers

bent-nose pliers or second pair of chain-nose pliers

flush cutters

These two bracelets may look very different, but they were created in the same way: They are completely crafted from materials I had an urge to play with right at that very minute! They were designed with pure spontaneity. The first was inspired by the beautiful ruby zoisite coins. The colors remind me of delicious watermelon. I just had to showcase these disks. I knew I had a great stone to start the design, and I just took off and enjoyed myself! For the second bracelet, I wanted to show off the impressive jasper bead to full effect. I combined the stone with a leather strap, as if the stone were to be worn as a watch, with the leather as the band. Adding rose quartz and the cubic zirconia charms made the piece more feminine. Follow my lead and see what you can create when you improvise.

RUBY COIN BRACELET

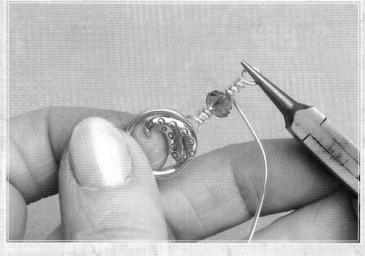

1. Attach clasp

Cut a 7" (18cm) piece of silver wire and wire wrap it to the round piece of the toggle clasp (see Techniques, page 17). Place a Tanzanite spacer bead on the wire and close the end with a wire wrap.

2. Connect ruby coins and chain

Wrap a 7" (18cm) piece of wire to the wrapped Tanzanite spacer bead. Place a ruby coin on the wire and close it with a wire wrap. Wrap a 7" (18cm) piece of wire to the ruby coin wrap and place a ruby coin on the wire. Wrap the free end of the wire to the textured and smooth cable chain.

3. Wire wrap dangles to chain

Place a Tanzanite spacer bead on a head pin and wire wrap it to the first smooth link of the chain. Repeat on the last smooth link of the chain. Place a Kambaba rondelle on a head pin and wire wrap it to the middle smooth link in the chain.

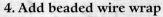

4. Add beaded wire wrap

Wrap an 8" (20cm) piece of wire to the end of the chain. Place the oval quartz bead, a Kambaba rondelle and a daisy bead on the wire and wrap it closed.

5. Attach clasp

Wrap a 7" (18cm) piece of wire to the bar of the toggle clasp. Place a Tanzanite spacer bead on the wire and wire wrap it to the open end of the last wrap on the bracelet.

RICE JASPER BRACELET

1. Crimp leather
Place a crimp tube on the end of the braided leather and crimp it tight with flat-nose pliers. Repeat on the other end.

2. Attach crystal dangles
Place a daisy spacer and a cubic zirconia bead on a head pin and wire wrap the dangle to the last link of the chain (see Techniques, pages 16–17). Repeat. Place a cubic zirconia bead and a daisy spacer on a head pin and wire wrap the dangle to the last link of the chain, between the two other cubic zirconia dangles.

3. Connect leather and chain
Wrap the silver wire to the chain. Place a daisy spacer, two rose quartz chips, a daisy spacer, the jasper rice bead, a bead cap facing toward the jasper rice bead, and a daisy spacer on the wire. Wrap the free end of the wire to the crimp on the end of the leather.

4. Attach clasp
To finish, attach the clasp to the free end of the leather with a jump ring.

Red Planet Necklace

MATERIALS

5 polymer clay art beads (EJR Beads)

18 4mm Light Siam AB Swarovski bicones

20 6mm Vitrail Medium Swarovski rounds

6 1" (3cm) pieces of black rubber tubing (Rio Grande)

1½ coils stainless steel memory wire, necklace size

1 sterling silver figure-eight clasp

8 22-gauge sterling silver head pins

18 18-gauge, 5mm ID sterling silver jump rings (Urban Maille)

66 18-gauge, 3.5mm ID sterling silver jump rings (Urban Maille)

8 8mm sterling silver jump rings

12 6mm sterling silver jump rings

TOOLS

round-nose pliers

round-nose pliers for memory wire

chain-nose pliers

bent-nose pliers or second pair of chain-nose pliers

flush cutters

flush cutters for memory wire

CREATIVE CONNECTION

EMMA RALPH

Emma Ralph creates unique art beads using polymer clay, ceramic and lampwork glass. A set of her polymer clay beads is featured in this necklace. To see more of her work, visit www.ejrbeads.co.uk

Q: What is something important you would like people to know about the creative process?

A: The creative process is not alchemy. It is not some strange magic that only a certain elite group is given. Everyone should welcome creativity into their lives, and recognize it when it is there. It's so sad when I hear people saying, "Oh I wish I was creative," because so often they don't realize they already are.

This wild orbit around your neck is meant to remind you of all things galaxy related! It goes around and around in many different ways. There are small and large chain maille flowers along with the mysterious color of Vitrail, and hot red Siam crystals. The unusual polymer clay beads, with their sparks and glow, look like little planets from outer space. I wanted to have them lie up close to the neck, so I used a clasp, which is unusual with memory wire. I like the way everything is spinning every which way on this necklace; the pattern on the beads, the little dangles and the progression of the colors against the black of the rubber tubing.

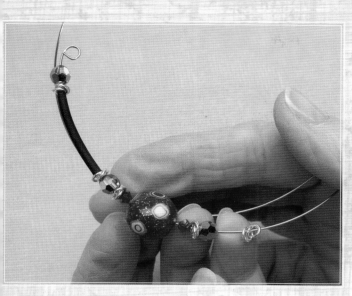

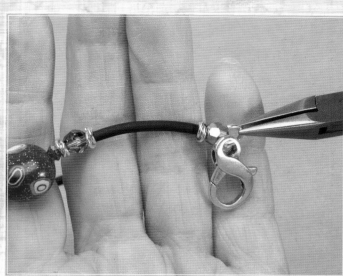

1. String beads

Make twenty-two 3-ring flowers from the 3.5mm ID jump rings (see Techniques, page 15). Make a loop at the end of the memory wire with round-nose pliers made for memory wire and string beads in the following pattern: Vitrail round, a flower, rubber tubing, a flower, Vitrail round, a flower, Siam bicone, polymer clay bead, Siam bicone and a flower. Repeat the pattern a total of five times, and end with a Vitrail round. Make a loop at the open end of the memory wire.

2. Add clasp

Place an 8mm jump ring on the loop at one end of the memory wire. Use a jump ring to connect the clasp to the loop at the other end of the necklace.

3. Create dangles

Place a Siam bicone and a Vitrail round on a head pin and wire wrap the dangle to a loop at the end of the necklace (see Techniques, pages 16–17). Repeat on the other end. Place a Siam bicone and a Vitrail round on a head pin and wire wrap it closed. Repeat to make a total of six crystal dangles. Make six 3-ring flowers using 5mm ID jump rings. Link a crystal dangle to a flower with two 6mm jump rings. Repeat for all dangles.

4. Attach dangles to necklace

Use 8mm jump rings to attach the dangles to the necklace, one over each piece of rubber tubing.

Naughty and Nice Bracelet

I had a ball designing this bracelet! I wanted the focus to be on the amusing word tags and wild clasp, so I kept the rest of this bracelet simple. The chain maille pattern is pleasing to the eye in its simplicity. It has a nice heft to it. And the shiny silver of all the components in this design is very eye-catching. Wearing this bracelet will let everyone know just what kind of mood you're in!

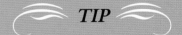

TIP

Consider making this as a necklace with the padlock as a focal. However, you have to have a bit of a sense of humor to carry it off.

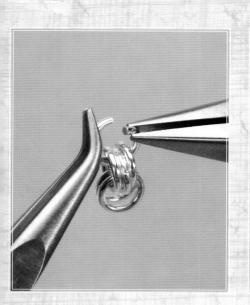

1. Connect jump rings

Hook an open 5mm ID jump ring through three closed 5mm ID jump rings and close it. Link a second and third jump ring to the three closed rings following the same path as the first (see Techniques, page 14).

2. Continue chain

Continue to add to the chain in the 3-in-3 ring pattern. Be careful not to scratch the jump rings as you learn the ins and outs of weaving the 3-in-3 pattern.

3. Add clasp

Once the chain is the length you desire, link an 8mm jump ring to each end. Place the clasp on one of the 8mm jump rings. Attach the message tag to the same jump ring with two 6mm jump rings.

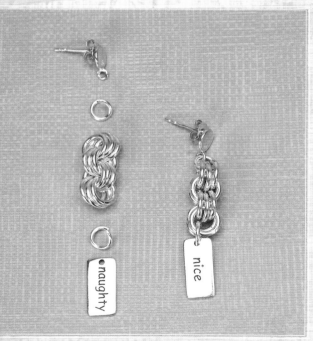

NAUGHTY AND NICE EARRINGS

Link 5mm ID jump rings together in the 3-in-3 pattern to create a piece of chain with four 3-ring units. Use a 6mm jump ring to attach the message tag to the end of the chain. Connect the free end of the chain to the earring post with a 6mm jump ring. Repeat for the second earring.

Sara Crewe Charm Bracelet

MATERIALS

CHARM BRACELET

11 iolite disk beads

19 6mm Sapphire AB Swarovski rounds

11 6mm Montana Swarovski rounds

8 blue batik lampwork saucer beads
(Alicia Abla)

57 sterling silver hex beads (The Bead Shop)

11 6mm sterling silver flower bead caps

14" (36cm) length of sterling silver textured
5-link chain (66 links)

7" (18cm) length of sterling silver antiqued
textured chain (39 links)

7" (18cm) length of sterling silver antiqued
twist chain (19 links)

1 sterling silver screw clasp (Urban Maille)

49 22-gauge sterling silver head pins

4 6mm sterling silver jump rings

4 8mm sterling silver jump rings

NECKLACE VARIATION

1 focal bead (Alicia Abla)

134 iolite disk beads

36 sterling silver hex beads (The Bead Shop)

2 6mm sterling silver flower bead caps

20" (51cm) strand of .019" (.48mm) 49-
strand wire

1 sterling silver screw clasp (Urban Maille)

2 sterling silver crimp tubes

This bracelet is inspired by a beautiful set of lampwork beads that reminds me of the patterns on oriental rugs. Studying them takes me back to a book I read over and over as a child, *A Little Princess* by Frances Hodgson Burnett. The main character, Sara Crewe, has many beautiful things when the story begins, but shortly loses everything. One day, exhausted and freezing, she trudges up to her drafty garret bedroom and finds it magically transformed, draped in luxurious oriental rugs, warm throws and pillows. I made this bracelet to reflect the exotic mood of the oriental rugs in the story, and the abundance of what awaited the little princess.

EARRING VARIATION

2 square focal beads (Alicia Abla)

2 iolite disk beads

2 sterling silver hex beads (The Bead Shop)

4 6mm kyanite rounds

4 6mm sterling silver flower bead caps

12" (30cm) piece of 18-gauge sterling silver wire

2 decorative sterling silver ear wires

2 22-gauge sterling silver head pins

BRACELET VARIATION

5 focal beads (Alicia Abla)

6 6mm kyanite rounds

2 6mm sterling silver flower bead caps

12" (30cm) strand of .019" (.48mm) 49-strand wire

1 sterling silver lobster clasp

1 lampwork inlay charm (Alicia Abla)

2 sterling silver crimp tubes

TOOLS

round-nose pliers

chain-nose pliers

bent-nose pliers or second pair of chain-nose pliers

flush cutters

flush cutters for beading wire

CREATIVE CHALLENGE

Did you have a favorite book or story as a child? Use your memories of that book or story to design a piece of jewelry. Then, reread that same story and design another piece of jewelry while it is still fresh in your mind. What new inspiration have you found now that you are grown up?

1. Attach iolite and Montana dangles

Cut the 5-link chain into two 7" (18cm) pieces. Slide a hex bead and an iolite disk bead onto a head pin. Use a bundled wire wrap to attach the beaded head pin to a smooth link in the chain that is next to a textured link (see Techniques, page 18). Repeat at the first smooth link before and after each textured link.

Slide a hex bead, a bead cap and a Montana round onto a head pin and wire wrap the dangle to a smooth link next to a textured link on the second piece of chain (see Techniques, pages 16–17). Repeat at the first smooth link before and after each textured link.

Make sure all of the dangles hang from the same side of the chain.

2. Attach Sapphire dangles

Slide a hex bead and a Sapphire AB round onto a head pin and wire wrap the dangle to the first link of the antiqued twist chain. Repeat on every link of the chain.

3. Attach lampwork beads

Place a hex bead, a lampwork bead and a hex bead on a head pin. Wire wrap the beaded head pin to the fifth link from the end of the antiqued textured chain. Repeat at every fourth link in the chain.

4. Attach clasp

Connect all four chains by hooking one 8mm jump ring through the last link of each chain; close the ring. The chains should be in the following order: Montana chain, lampwork chain, Sapphire AB chain, iolite chain. Hook a second 8mm jump ring through the four chains, following the same path as the first. Repeat at the other end.

Attach the clasp to the 8mm jump rings with two 6mm jump rings at each end (see Techniques, page 14).

SARA CREWE NECKLACE

Use a crimp tube to crimp half of the clasp to the end of the 49-strand wire (see Techniques, page 19). String the beads onto the wire in the following order: one hex bead, nineteen iolite disk beads, twenty hex beads, twenty iolite disk beads, one hex bead, twenty iolite disk beads, five hex beads, one bead cap, the focal bead, one bead cap, five hex beads, twenty iolite disk beads, one hex bead, fifteen iolite disk beads, one hex bead, twenty iolite disk beads, one hex bead, twenty iolite disk beads and one hex bead. Crimp the second half of the clasp to the free end of the wire.

SARA CREWE EARRINGS

Wire wrap the end of a 6" (15cm) piece of silver wire closed (see Techniques, page 17). Place a bead cap, a kyanite round, a focal bead, a kyanite round and a bead cap on the wire and close the free end with a wire wrap. Place an iolite disk bead and a hex bead on a head pin and link the dangle to the focal dangle with a bundled wire wrap (see Techniques, page 18). Open the ear wire, place the free end of the focal dangle on the ear wire, and close it. Repeat for the second earring.

SARA CREWE BRACELET

Crimp the charm that will serve as half of the clasp to the end of the 49-strand wire (see Techniques, page 19). Place a bead cap on the wire and string beads in the following pattern: kyanite round, focal bead. Repeat four more times, ending with a kyanite round. Add a bead cap and crimp the free end of the wire to the lobster claw clasp.

Gigi Bracelet

I have a secret: I love charm bracelets! When I was a little girl, I would beg to look at my mother's and grandmothers' charm bracelets. I am crazy about examining the tiny treasures you discover when you look closely at fabulous, imaginative charm bracelets. I have made all sorts of charm bracelets, and this one was inspired by the 1980s. This bracelet has so many different elements that I had to work hard to unite them. I used heart shapes throughout the design and used a limited color palette. And then I literally tied it all together with a bow! Try this design, or adapt it by collecting some of the beads you have at home to make your own treasure bracelet.

MATERIALS

3 7mm white freshwater pearls

2 4mm gold-filled stardust rounds

1 6mm sterling silver stardust round

9 3mm Crystal AB Swarovski rounds

2 13mm foiled heart beads (Venetian Bead Shop)

1 8mm faceted champagne cubic zirconia round

1 8mm faceted pink cubic zirconia round

1 8mm faceted crystal cubic zirconia round

1 6mm × 9mm Rose Swarovski teardrop

1 6mm × 9mm Crystal AB Swarovski teardrop

1 antiqued gold-plated XOXO charm

1 antiqued gold-plated spiral heart charm

1 antiqued gold-plated cordial heart charm

1 small sterling silver flower charm (the one shown here is half of a clasp by Green Girl Studios)

1 sterling silver beaded heart charm

1 sterling silver heart-and-key charm

2 sterling silver doodle heart bead frames (Penny Michelle)

1 sterling silver tiny heart charm

26-link section of 6.5mm gold-filled cable chain

48-link section of 5mm sterling silver rolo chain

1 antiqued gold-plated 2-strand toggle clasp

3 26-gauge sterling silver head pins

2 22-gauge sterling silver head pins

7 24-gauge sterling silver head pins

3 6mm gold-filled jump rings

8 8mm sterling silver jump rings

1 4mm sterling silver jump ring

16" (41cm) piece of "Ooh la la" ribbon (The Ribbon Jar)

All charms are from Fusion Beads unless otherwise noted.

TOOLS

round-nose pliers

chain-nose pliers

bent-nose pliers or second pair of chain-nose pliers

flush cutters

scissors

1. Attach charms to gold-filled chain

Attach the charms to the gold-filled chain in the following locations with gold-filled jump rings, counting links from left to right: at the 3rd link, the gold-plated XOXO charm; at the 5th link, the gold-plated spiral heart charm; at the 7th link, the gold-plated cordial heart charm. Wire wrap the following dangles to the gold-filled chain in the following locations, again counting links from left to right: at the 11th link, on a 22-gauge head pin, a Crystal AB round, a foiled heart bead and a Crystal AB round; at the 13th link, on a 24-gauge head pin, a gold-filled stardust round and a Crystal AB round; at the 15th link, on a 24-gauge head pin, a champagne cubic zirconia round and a Crystal AB round; at the 19th link, on a 22-gauge head pin, a Crystal AB round, a foiled heart bead and a Crystal AB round; at the 23rd link, on a 26-gauge head pin, a gold-filled stardust round and a pearl (see Techniques, pages 16–17).

2. Attach charms to silver chain

Attach the charms to the silver chain in the following locations with 8mm silver jump rings, counting links from left to right: at the 9th link, the silver flower charm; at the 13th link, the beaded silver heart charm; at the 17th link, the heart-and-key silver charm. Wire wrap the following dangles to the silver chain in the following locations, again counting links from left to right: at the 5th link, on a 24-gauge head pin, a Crystal AB round and a silver stardust round; at the 23rd link, on a 24-gauge head pin, the pink cubic zirconia round inside of a heart bead frame; at the 29th link, on a 24-gauge head pin, the Crystal teardrop inside of a heart bead frame; at the 33rd link, on a 24-gauge head pin, a crystal cubic zirconia round; at the 39th link, on a 26-gauge head pin, a pearl; at the 43rd link, on a 24-gauge head pin, a Rose teardrop and a Crystal AB round. Wire wrap a Crystal AB round and a pearl on a 26-gauge head pin to the silver flower charm. Attach the tiny heart charm to the pink cubic zirconia and heart frame dangle with a 4mm jump ring.

3. Attach clasp

Hook an 8mm jump ring through the last link of the gold-filled chain and through the top loop of the toggle clasp and close it. Repeat with the silver chain on the bottom loop of the clasp. Repeat on the opposite end of both chains.

4. Add ribbon

Tie the ribbon in a bow and trim the ends neatly. Use an 8mm jump ring to connect the bow to the round piece of the toggle clasp.

Pictograph Bracelet

MATERIALS

BRACELET

1 large lampwork tab bead (Kim Miles)

2 sterling silver daisy spacer beads

9" (23cm) piece of 18-gauge dead soft sterling silver wire

1 leopard-patterned sterling silver box clasp (Nina Designs)

76 14-gauge, 5mm ID sterling silver jump rings (Urban Maille)

8 6mm sterling silver jump rings

EARRING VARIATION

2 12mm lampwork spacer beads (Kim Miles)

4 sterling silver daisy spacer beads

2 leopard-patterned sterling silver ear wires (Nina Designs)

2 22-gauge sterling silver head pins

28 14-gauge, 5mm ID sterling silver jump rings (Urban Maille)

4 8mm sterling silver jump rings

TOOLS

round-nose pliers

chain-nose pliers

bent-nose pliers or second pair of chain-nose pliers

flush cutters

I wanted to create something really great with this brilliantly colored lampwork bead. I used the pictograph of a goat on the focal bead as the inspiration for my design. Because of the natural, animal look of the goat, I selected the leopard-patterned box clasp. I thought the Byzantine chain maille pattern in a hefty gauge would be appropriate for such a large bead with a cool, ancient-looking design. This goat reminded me of prehistoric cave drawings, and the Byzantine design itself is very old. They were easily drawn together. Bring out the animal in yourself and try a project like this!

1. Begin chain

Hook an open 5mm ID jump ring through two closed 5mm ID jump rings and close it. Link a second open jump ring through the two closed jump rings, following the same path as the first ring, and close it (see Techniques, page 14).

Hook an open jump ring through the two newly added rings and close it. Add another jump ring, following the same path as the first ring, and close it, creating a piece of chain with three 2-ring units.

2. Fold down rings

Let the two top rings fall to the sides of the two middle rings.

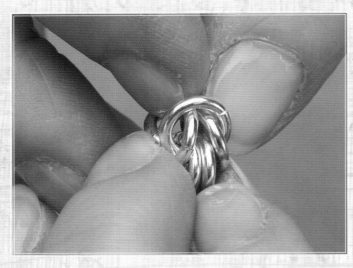

3. Push rings up

Push the two fallen rings inward and up.

4. Turn unit and part rings

Turn the chain 90° between your fingers and spread apart the two rings facing you. You will now have a side view of the two fallen rings that you have pushed inward and up.

5. Attach jump rings

Hook a jump ring through the two fallen rings you have pushed inward and up. Close the newly added jump ring and add a second jump ring, following the same path as the first. This completes the first unit of chain.

6. Begin second section of chain

Place two closed jump rings on an open jump ring and hook the open ring through the last two rings on the chain.

7. Finish chain pieces

Hook a second jump ring through all four rings, following the same path as the first. Repeat Steps 2–5 to build a second unit of chain. Add a third unit of chain to the bracelet.

Build a second 3-unit section of chain for the second half of the bracelet.

8. Join chain pieces and bead

Wire wrap one end of the silver wire closed, then place a daisy spacer bead, the tab bead, and a daisy spacer bead on the wire (see Techniques, page 17). Close the end of the wire with a wire wrap. Hook a 6mm jump ring through the wire wrap and the end of a piece of chain and close the jump ring. Attach a second jump ring, following the path of the first. Repeat on the other side of the wire wrap.

9. Attach clasp

Hook a 6mm jump ring through the clasp and the free end of a piece of chain and close it. Attach a second jump ring, following the path of the first. Repeat on the other side of the bracelet.

PICTOGRAPH EARRINGS

Create a 2-unit secion of chain. Place a daisy spacer bead, a lampwork spacer bead and a daisy spacer bead on a head pin and wire wrap the dangle closed (see Techniques, pages 16–17). Link the wire wrap to the chain with an 8mm jump ring. Attach the ear wire to the free end of the chain with an 8mm jump ring. Repeat for the second earring.

Mandala Earrings

MATERIALS

8 6mm Light Peach AB Swarovski rounds

4 6mm Crystal AB Swarovski rounds

4 4mm Crystal Golden Shadow Swarovski bicones

4 4mm Light Peach AB Swarovski bicones

4 4mm Light Azore Swarovski bicones

2 38mm Cloud Swarovski Rhodium filigree components

12" (30cm) piece of 22-gauge dead soft sterling silver wire

2 sterling silver ear wires

22 24-gauge sterling silver head pins

2 sterling silver bangle bracelets (Fusion Beads)

TOOLS

round-nose pliers

chain-nose pliers

bent-nose pliers or second pair of chain-nose pliers

flush cutters

Mandalas are geometric figures representing the universe in Hindu and Buddhist symbolism, and I am attracted to them for many reasons, including their meditative and restorative qualities. In most cases, mandalas are circular—an iconic shape that asks you to understand, to the utmost of your capabilities, that life began and will go on beyond what we presently perceive. If there is no beginning, there is no end. My friend Rae creates mandalas of all sorts that I really admire, and I decided to commission her to make a mandala card for my online jewelry company to include with special purchases. The card unfolds into two halves that prop up the little mandala altar depicted on the card. These earrings were inspired by Rae and the mandalas she creates. Make them, enjoy them and walk in beauty.

1. Attach dangles

Place a Light Peach bicone on a head pin and wire wrap it to the Cloud component (see Techniques, pages 16–17). Continue wire wrapping beads to consecutive loops on the Cloud component in the following order: a Crystal Golden Shadow bicone, a Light Azore bicone, a Light Peach round, a Crystal AB round, a Light Peach round, a Crystal AB round, a Light Peach round, a Light Azore bicone, a Crystal Golden Shadow bicone and a Light Peach bicone.

2. Attach bangle

Wire wrap the end of a 6" (15cm) piece of wire to the Cloud component, opposite the middle Light Peach round. Place a Light Peach round on the wire and wrap the free end of the wire to the silver bangle.

3. Attach ear wire

Open the ear wire and hook it through the same loop on the bangle as the Cloud component. Close the ear wire. Repeat Steps 1–3 for the second earring.

Edward the Sheep Bracelet

MATERIALS

1 sterling silver enameled button (Gita Maria)

4 sterling silver enameled burgundy heart charms (Gita Maria)

4 sterling silver enameled purple heart charms (Gita Maria)

5 sterling silver enameled rose heart charms (Gita Maria)

5 16mm wavy sterling silver rings (The Bead Shop)

1 10mm sterling silver lobster claw clasp

21 6mm sterling silver jump rings

TOOLS

chain-nose pliers

bent-nose pliers or second pair of chain-nose pliers

This great little bracelet came about because of a funny memory. I have an e-mail friendship with a bead artist, Emma Ralph. Emma and I, along with her family, used to watch sheep on a live webcam located at the Loch Ness. Emma's family named one of the sheep Edward. While everyone else was watching for "Nessie," we were gripped by the travails, joys and dramas of Edward. This enamel button, depicting a little sheep with a big heart, reminded me of Edward. I chose enameled heart links to coordinate with Edward, but they were too small to hold their own. I added the wavy jump rings to balance the design. This bracelet is the perfect reminder of the fun we had watching Edward wander about in his field near the Loch Ness.

1. Begin chain

Hook a jump ring through the loop on the back of the button and through a burgundy heart charm. Close the jump ring. Use a jump ring to connect a purple heart charm to the burgundy heart charm. Use a jump ring to connect a rose heart charm to the purple heart charm. Contine to add heart charms, repeating the burgundy, purple, rose pattern three more times.

2. Add clasp

Hook a jump ring through the loop on the back of the button and through a rose heart charm. Link a chain of two more jump rings to the other side of the rose heart charm. Use a jump ring to connect the lobster claw clasp to the long end of the chain.

3. Add wavy rings

Pull a wavy ring over the long end of the bracelet chain. Link the wavy ring to the bracelet with a jump ring between the first rose heart and the second burgundy heart. Attach wavy rings at every second jump ring.

Sleek Squares Bracelet

MATERIALS

1 39mm square sterling silver toggle clasp
(Via Murano)

176 18-gauge, 4.5mm ID sterling silver jump
rings (Urban Maille)

4 6mm sterling silver jump rings

TOOLS

chain-nose pliers

bent-nose pliers or second pair
of chain-nose pliers

The box chain weave creates sleek, slinky chains. Unadorned, they make very modern jewelry. However, their simplicity also makes them a great backdrop for other design elements. When I found this striking clasp, I wanted to display it prominently. I chose to pair this knockout clasp with a box chain because the square shape of each element enhances the other. Even though this bracelet is unadorned by gemstones or beads, it makes a memorable impression. What would you display on this sleek chain?

TIP

This weave sometimes goes off in two directions. You have to take charge of the direction your bracelet is going by holding it vertically once in a while as you weave it. Look at it from that vantage point and see if it is going in one direction. Continue to coax it in the direction you are aiming for by running your fingers over the chain. Remember, you want a square box look going in just one direction.

1. Begin chain

Hook an open 4.5mm ID jump ring through two closed 4.5mm ID jump rings and close it. Link a second open jump ring through the two closed jump rings, following the same path as the first ring, and close it (see Techniques, page 14).

Hook an open jump ring through the two newly added rings and close it. Add another jump ring, following the same path as the first ring, and close it, creating a piece of chain with three 2-ring units.

2. Fold down rings

Let the two top rings fall to the sides of the two middle rings.

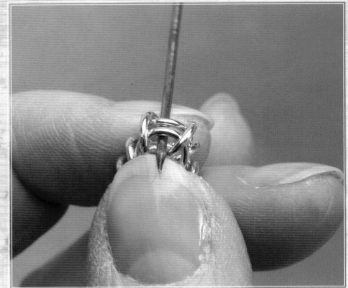

3. Push rings up

Push the two fallen rings inward and up.

4. Turn unit and part rings

Turn the chain 90° between your fingers and spread apart the two rings facing you. You now have a side view of the two fallen rings that you pushed inward and up.

Place two closed jump rings on an open jump ring and hook it through the two fallen rings that you pushed inward and up. The path the open jump ring should take is shown here by a pointer.

Close the open jump ring and add a second following the same path as the first.

5. Fold down rings

Again, let the top two rings fall to the sides of the chain.

6. Push rings up

Push the two fallen rings inward and up.

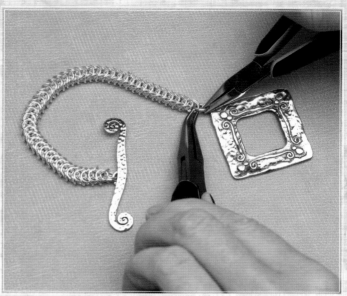

7. Turn unit and part rings

Turn the chain 90° and spread apart the two rings facing you, exposing the fallen rings. Place two closed jump rings on an open jump ring and hook it through the two fallen rings that you pushed inward and up. Close the open jump ring and add a second following the same path as the first. Repeat Steps 5–7 until all rings are used, or until the bracelet is the length you desire.

8. Add clasp

Attach the toggle clasp to the ends of the bracelet with two 6mm jump rings on each end.

CREATIVE CHALLENGE

Go to an antique store. Spend the afternoon studying the design elements, such as shape and color, that were used during different eras. Use these elements to design a piece of jewelry reminiscent of a certain time period.

Diamond Choker

MATERIALS

2 12" (30cm) lengths of 4mm black suede lace

138 18-gauge, 3.5mm ID copper jump rings (Urban Maille)

45 blue rubber rings (The Ring Lord)

45 black rubber rings (The Ring Lord)

TOOLS

chain-nose pliers

bent-nose pliers or second pair of chain-nose pliers

TIP

This pattern could also be used for a bracelet. I suggest using the suede lace to tie the bracelet closed. It's a good look, plus it will hold the rubber rings firmly on the wrist. It will look a bit like a cuff.

This is a fun project if you enjoy exploring different directions in your jewelry design. Instead of traditional metal rings for this choker, I chose rubber rings. The Japanese chain maille pattern has its roots firmly in the past, but using the rubber rings brought the pattern right up to the minute. I like the combination of the blue and black rings, arranged and accented by the shiny copper rings. There are so many variations to make this necklace unique to you. Experiment with rubber colors or make this design with traditional metal rings. Switch out the copper rings for a different metal, or add dangles to the bottom of the chain maille units. Put your own stamp on this design!

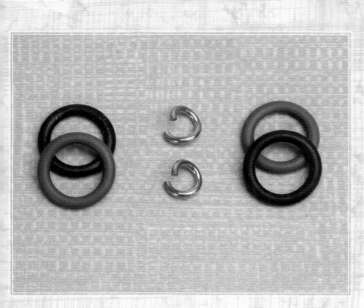

1. Prepare components

To begin, place a blue ring on top of a black ring (blue unit) and a black ring on top of a blue ring (black unit). Open two copper jump rings.

2. Join rings

Place one copper jump ring through all four rubber rings and close it. It will be a snug fit. Place the second copper ring next to the first and close it (see Techniques, page 14).

3. Continue adding rings

Place a black ring on top of a blue ring and connect them to the blue unit from Steps 1–2 with two copper rings. Place a blue ring on top of a black ring and connect them to the black unit from Steps 1–2 with two copper rings. Place a blue ring on top of a black ring and connect to both black units in the previous row. Place a blue ring on top of a black ring and connect to the black unit added previously in this step with two copper jump rings. Repeat, adding a row with two black units and a row with one blue unit to form a diamond.

4. Join diamonds

Create four more diamonds following Steps 1–3. Join the diamonds with two copper jump rings as shown. If you like, flip over every other diamond so that two diamonds have black units at the tips and three units have blue units at the tips. Alternate the units when connecting.

5. Attach suede laces

Pull a length of suede lace through the last unit of rubber rings. Double over and close with five copper rings. Repeat on the opposite side.

Art House Bracelet

MATERIALS

BRACELET

6 lampwork art beads (EJR Beads)

6 lampwork spacer beads (EJR Beads)

18 3mm seamless sterling silver beads

1 sterling silver lobster claw clasp

6 22-gauge sterling silver head pins

6 27mm textured sterling silver rings
(Via Murano)

15 ½" (13mm) square antiqued brass jump
rings (Ornamentea)

8 8mm sterling silver jump rings

EARRING VARIATION

2 lampwork art beads (EJR Beads)

2 lampwork spacer beads (EJR Beads)

6 3mm seamless sterling silver beads

2 decorative earring posts (Nina Designs)

2 22-gauge sterling silver head pins

2 27mm textured sterling silver rings
(Via Murano)

8 ½" (13mm) square antiqued brass jump
rings (Ornamentea)

2 4mm sterling silver jump rings

2 8mm sterling silver jump rings

TOOLS

round-nose pliers

chain-nose pliers

bent-nose pliers or second pair of chain-
nose pliers

flush cutters

This fascinating set of lampwork beads has undeniable vibrance! Because it is alive with color and movement, I wanted to showcase the set in a very dramatic way. The framing I created with large sterling hammered circles and brass squares is very unusual, but it complements the beads. The different shapes work well together to balance the design. This bold bracelet has a lot of appeal. If you come across a set of stunning lampwork beads, try a design like this to bring out every aspect of their artful charm.

1. Join rings

Hook a brass jump ring through two silver rings and close it. Add a second and third brass jump ring following the same path as the first. Attach the remaining silver rings and brass jump rings to form a chain.

2. Attach beaded dangles

Place a silver bead, a lampwork spacer bead, a silver bead, a lampwork art bead and a silver bead on a head pin. Wire wrap the dangle closed (see Techniques, pages 16–17). Hook an 8mm jump ring through the first silver ring on the bracelet and through a beaded dangle. Close the jump ring. Repeat, attaching one beaded dangle to each silver ring. Hang all of the dangles from the same side of the chain.

3. Attach clasp

Hook an 8mm jump ring through the lobster claw clasp and the first silver ring on the bracelet. Close the jump ring. Hook an 8mm jump ring through the last ring on the bracelet and close.

ART HOUSE EARRINGS

Hook a 4mm jump ring through the loop at the bottom of the earring post and close it. Connect the 4mm jump ring and a silver ring with a single square brass jump ring. Hook three brass jump rings through the sterling ring. Place a silver bead, a lampwork spacer bead, a silver bead, a lampwork art bead and a silver bead on a head pin. Wire wrap the beaded head pin closed (see Techniques, pages 16–17). Hook an 8mm jump ring through the beaded dangle and through the three brass jump rings at the bottom of the earring. Close the jump ring. Repeat for the second earring.

Ancient Armor Bracelet

MATERIALS

1 square toggle clasp

230 16-gauge, 4mm ID Argentium sterling silver jump rings (Urban Maille)

6 8mm sterling silver jump rings

TOOLS

chain-nose pliers

bent-nose pliers or second pair of chain-nose pliers

European four-in-one mesh is an ancient chain maille pattern I updated here by using Argentium sterling silver jump rings and a metal clay clasp. I fell in love with metal clay a few years ago. I loved the freedom it gave me. I loved creating this clasp with such an up-to-date material to add a twist to a historic chain maille pattern. I added cubic zirconia to the clasp to give it a bit of flash, but otherwise I let the chain maille shine in this design. And the chain maille will continue to shine because it is made with Argentium sterling silver, a new type of sterling silver that is almost tarnish-free. Don't be afraid to try new materials and techniques, but don't abandon your old standbys. Try them together and see what happens!

1. Join rings

Place four closed Argentium jump rings on one open ring and close it. Pinch two of the closed rings between your fingers and let the rest hang in a chain. The rings should form a 2-1-2 pattern.

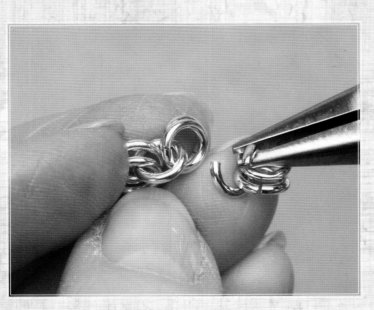

2. Continue adding rings

Place two closed Argentium rings on one open ring. Hook the open ring through the two top Argentium rings from the unit formed in Step 1. Close the open ring.

3. Arrange rings

Pinch the two newly added rings between your fingers and let the rest hang in a chain. The rings should now form a 2-1-2-1-2 pattern. Lay the chain flat so that pairs of rings on the ends and in the middle overlap like scales, as shown. The orientation of the rings is very important in this chain maille pattern, so make sure each ring is in the proper position before continuing.

4. Continue adding rings in pattern

Open an Argetium jump ring and hook it down through the bottom left ring and up through the bottom middle ring. Place two closed rings on the open ring and close it.

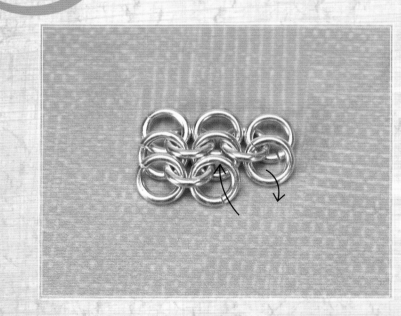

5. Continue chain

Arrange the newly added rings to follow the orientation of the chain. Open a jump ring and hook it through the chain, following the path of the arrow in the picture: down through the bottom ring in the middle row and down through the ring above it in the same row, then up through the last ring in the right row. Place a closed ring on the open jump ring and close it.

6. Finish chain

Arrange the newly added rings so they follow the pattern made by the other rings. Repeat Steps 4–5 until all of the rings are used or until the bracelet is the length you desire.

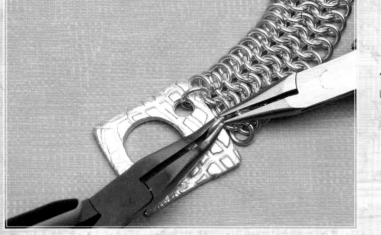

7. Attach clasp

Use two 8mm jump rings to attach the clasp to the bracelet.

Trio of Sparkling Earrings

MATERIALS

ON-THE-SQUARE EARRINGS

2 6mm Black Diamond Swarovski cubes

2 6mm Crystal Silver Shade Swarovski cubes

2 6mm Vitrail Medium Swarovski cubes

2 18mm × 24mm square sterling silver chandelier components (Fusion Beads)

12" (30cm) section of sterling 3.5mm round link chain

2 flat French sterling silver ear wires with bead

6 22-gauge sterling silver head pins

6 4mm sterling silver jump rings

GOLDEN FLOWERS EARRINGS

2 6mm × 9mm Jet AB Swarovski teardrops

2 4mm Light Colorado Topaz AB Swarovski rounds

2 10mm Light Colorado Topaz Swarovski flower links

2 10mm Colorado Topaz Swarovski flower links

2 10mm Smoky Topaz Swarovski flower links

4 vermeil star bead caps

2 gold-filled French ear wires with bead

2 24-gauge Smoky Topaz Swarovski head pins

4 6mm gold-filled jump rings

I love Swarovski crystals—who doesn't? I gave myself free reign to design some purely pretty earrings in three distinctly different styles. I know any one of these pairs of earrings would make a great addition to an earring lover's collection. Each pair was designed with a very carefully thought-out pattern in mind. You can start with a color, component or finding when you want to design a pair of earrings. I chose to start with Swarovski crystals, but I could have focused on another type of bead and enjoyed the challenge just as well. Thinking it through is the fun part!

LOOPING DECO EARRINGS

2 6mm × 9mm Crystal AB Swarovski teardrops

2 6mm Rose Alabaster Swarovski rounds

2 5mm Light Rose Rhodium-plated Swarovski rondelles

2 18mm × 28mm sterling silver 6-loop chandelier components (Fusion Beads)

14-link section of 6mm Rose Swarovski round linked Rhodium channel chain

10-link section of 6mm Jet Swarovski round linked Rhodium channel chain

2 16mm sterling silver lever-back ear wires with tulip

2 24-gauge sterling silver head pins

8 4mm sterling silver jump rings

TOOLS

round-nose pliers

chain-nose pliers

bent-nose pliers or second pair of chain-nose pliers

flush cutters

ON-THE-SQUARE EARRINGS

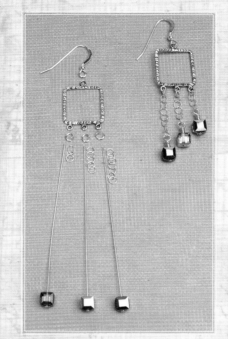

Cut a 4-link section of chain, a 5-link section of chain and a 7-link section of chain. Using jump rings, attach the chains, longest to shortest, to the loops at the bottom of the square chandelier component. Place a Black Diamond cube on a head pin and wire wrap it to the last link of the 4-link chain (see Techniques, pages 16–17). Place a Crystal Silver Shade cube on a head pin and wire wrap it to the last link of the 5-link chain. Place a Vitrail Medium cube on a head pin and wire wrap it to the last link of the 7-link chain. Open the ear wire and link it to the top loop of the square chandelier. Repeat for the second earring, mirroring chain and bead positions.

GOLDEN FLOWERS EARRINGS

Slide a bead cap, a Jet AB teardrop, a bead cap and a Light Topaz AB round onto a Smoky Topaz head pin. Wire wrap the beaded head pin to the Smoky Topaz flower link (see Techniques, pages 16–17). Use a jump ring to connect a Colorado Topaz flower link to the free end of the Smoky Topaz flower link. Connect the Light Colorado Topaz flower link to the Colorado Topaz flower link with a jump ring. Open the ear wire and hook it through the Light Colorado Topaz flower link. Close the ear wire. Repeat for the second earring.

CREATIVE CHALLENGE

Listen to the work of a composer you have never heard before. Try classical music for the first time, or go back to it. Close your eyes while you listen. Does the music bring certain colors, shapes or textures to mind? Use these elements in your next design.

LOOPING DECO EARRINGS

1. Create beaded dangle

Place a Crystal AB teardrop, a Light Rose rondelle, and a Rose Alabaster round on a head pin and wire wrap it to the middle loop of the chandelier component (see Techniques, pages 16–17).

2. Attach chains

Use a jump ring to connect five links of the Jet chain to the chandelier component on the loop to the left of the center dangle. Connect the free end of the chain to the chandelier component on the loop to the right of the beaded dangle with a jump ring. Repeat with seven links of the Rose chain on the outside loops of the chandelier.

3. Attach ear wire

Open the ear wire and hook it through the top loop on the chandelier component. Close the ear wire. Repeat Steps 1–3 for the second earring.

COLOR

How does color affect you? Do you have a favorite color? Colors have so many meanings: Green brings the freshness of spring to mind, but it is also the color of money; blue can be peaceful and serene, or the color of sadness; red can connote passion, power or joy. No matter how hard I try, there is no color on earth I can think of that doesn't already exist. That is pretty impressive! I am considering black and white as colors here, even though you and I know that they are actually either the absence of color or the presence of every color together, respectively. And by the way, where were you when you first found that out? And were you as disturbed by this revelation? I was!

I spend a lot of time thinking about color. It *always* plays a major part in my designs. I like my colors to dance with each other! My charm bracelets, such as Gigi (page 88), are good examples of colors playing well together. I made them endlessly at one point, and I never lost interest in them, because the color story was the point of each bracelet. They may have similarities, but they are not the same. Each one is unique, due to color choices I made.

For this chapter, I made three necklace designs, each with an additional design challenge I set for myself, just for fun. These three necklaces are totally different from each other, but all have color as the main point. When I was finished creating, I went back and redesigned them in different sets of colors so you could see what happens to a design when the color of the piece is changed. What a difference! Take a look at these projects and see the impact color alone has upon design.

115

Rainbow Ruffles Necklace

MATERIALS

RAINBOW RUFFLES NECKLACE

22 ruffled borosilicate lampwork beads in a variety of colors (Redside Designs)

24 5mm Swarovski bicones in colors to coordinate with the lampwork beads

135 sterling silver barbell spacer beads

30" (76cm) strand of .019" (.48mm) 49-strand wire

1 sterling silver toggle clasp

4 sterling silver crimp tubes

BLUE AND GREEN RUFFLES NECKLACE

22 ruffled borosilicate lampwork beads in blue and green shades (Redside Designs)

24 5mm Swarovski bicones in colors to coordinate with the lampwork beads

135 sterling silver barbell spacer beads

30" (76cm) strand of .019" (.48mm) 49-strand wire

1 sterling silver toggle clasp

4 sterling silver crimp tubes

TOOLS

chain-nose pliers

flush cutters for beading wire

This necklace celebrates color, femininity and light. The nature of borosilicate glass really shines through in these ruffled beads: The fumed and smoky appearance is alluring and unmistakable. I could have made a fabulous necklace design simply by stringing these rainbow beads together with barely any space between them, but I thought I would try something different. I took sterling Thai spacers and stacked them in sets of three on both sides of each ruffle bead. This opened up the design and let some serious air in! You can really admire each individual ruffle bead. I chose complementary Swarovski crystals for each ruffle, and ended the necklace with a wavy sterling toggle clasp similar to the ruffles. If you were to make a necklace similar to one of these, how would you plan it out?

CREATIVE CHALLENGE

Use writing to find inspiration. Try putting the story of your life into words. Write about your dreams, about what is important to you and about the things you love. Translate these thoughts into a fantastic, one-of-a-kind piece of jewelry just for you.

1. Crimp wire to clasp
Attach the 49-strand wire to the toggle clasp with a beaded double crimp using a crystal bicone (see Techniques, page 19).

2. String necklace
String beads onto the wire in the following pattern: three spacer beads, one lampwork bead, three spacer beads and one crystal bicone. Repeat twenty-two times, ending with three spacer beads.

3. Finish necklace
Finish the necklace by attaching the toggle clasp to the free end of the wire with a beaded double crimp.

BLUE AND GREEN RUFFLES NECKLACE

For this necklace, I limited my color scheme to green and blue. The sense of depth is enhanced, even though I strung the necklace in the same manner, using the same Thai spacers and Swarovski crystals. I also have two clear crystal ruffles in the necklace. Finding a place for them was my challenge to myself. I decided to place them in the middle of the necklace, and I like the way they flow with the design. The clear crystal ruffles make the necklace look rich because they are so there, even if they are clear.

Sun and Shadow Necklace

MATERIALS

SUN AND SHADOW NECKLACE

4 18mm Crystal AB Swarovski rondelles

4 18mm Crystal Silver Shade Swarovski rondelles

14 6mm × 10mm sterling silver disk beads

12 4mm × 5mm sterling silver hex beads (The Bead Shop)

100 24kt white gold-plated seed beads

1 8mm × 11mm × 37mm sterling silver face bead (Fusion Beads)

1 fine silver dangle (Kate McKinnon)

28" (71cm) strand of .019" (.48mm) 49-strand wire

5½" (14cm) piece of 22-gauge dead soft sterling silver wire

1 sterling silver hook-and-eye clasp with chain

4 sterling silver crimp tubes

ECLIPSE NECKLACE

4 18mm Crystal AB Swarovski rondelles

4 18mm Jet Swarovski rondelles

8 6mm × 10mm sterling silver disk beads

20 6mm seamless sterling silver rounds

50 matte black seed beads

50 mercury seed beads

1 8mm × 11mm × 37mm sterling silver face bead (Fusion Beads)

1 fine silver dangle (Kate McKinnon)

28" (71cm) strand of .019" (.48mm) 49-strand wire

5½" (14cm) piece of 22-gauge dead soft sterling silver wire

1 sterling silver hook-and-eye clasp with chain

4 sterling silver crimp tubes

TOOLS

round-nose pliers

chain-nose pliers

bent-nose pliers or second pair of chain-nose pliers

flush cutters

flush cutters for beading wire

I wanted to examine a minimal difference in color with a two-color necklace. To make it work, I needed an appropriate pendant. I liked the sterling face bead because of its cryptic appearance. The face bead is rectangular, long and somewhat unusual. On one side, the Crystal AB rondelles make up the "Sun" side of this split necklace and have a very dramatic and shiny presence. The opposite side, "Shadow," is made up of Crystal Silver Shade Swarovski rondelles, a more elusive color. Those giant rondelles reflect the light from all angles and the colors keep your eyes moving about, even though the difference is barely detectable. Try a color study of your own with a necklace like this.

1. Create dangle

Wire wrap the silver wire to the fine silver dangle (see Techniques, page 17). Place the face bead on the wire and close the free end with a wire wrap.

2. String necklace

Place the focal bead dangle on the 49-strand wire, followed by a hex bead, a disk bead, a Crystal AB rondelle and a disk bead. Repeat this pattern twice, then add a hex bead, a disk bead, a Crystal AB round, a hex bead and fifty seed beads. Repeat on the other side of the focal dangle, substituting Crystal Silver Shade rondelles for the Crystal AB rondelles.

3. Crimp wire to clasp

Use crimp tubes to crimp the clasp to the necklace with a double crimp on both ends of the wire (see Techniques, page 19).

ECLIPSE NECKLACE

This design is stark and strong, a change from the subtlety of the Sun and Shadow Necklace. The challenge I set for myself was to see if I could make a successful necklace with such an extremely noticeable color change. To make this design cohesive, I changed the seed beads, adding some balance to the new color layout. I used matte black seed beads with the Jet rondelles and mercury seed beads with the Crystal AB rondelles. I also preferred the sleekness of seamless silver rounds for this version of the necklace.

119

Electric Purple Necklace

MATERIALS

ELECTRIC PURPLE NECKLACE

60 12mm square purple turquoise beads

10 4mm Purple Velvet Swarovski rounds

8 sterling silver barbell spacer beads

38 DK Rose Luster seed beads

1 hammered fine silver ring charm
(Kate McKinnon)

1 fine silver heart charm (Kate McKinnon)

2 wavy sterling silver spacer bars
(Fusion Beads)

2 28" (71cm) strands of .019" (.48mm)
49-strand wire

1 fine silver toggle clasp (Kate McKinnon)

2 22-gauge sterling silver head pins

2 6mm sterling silver jump rings

4 sterling silver crimp tubes

LACE NECKLACE

65 10mm crazy lace agate rounds

14 6mm Dorado Swarovski rounds

4 sterling silver bamboo charms

2 wavy sterling silver spacer bars
(Fusion Beads)

2 28" (71cm) strands of .019" (.48mm)
49-strand wire

1 fine silver toggle clasp (Kate McKinnon)

6 24-gauge sterling silver head pins

4 sterling silver crimp tubes

TOOLS

round-nose pliers

chain-nose pliers

bent-nose pliers or second pair of chain-
nose pliers

flush cutters

flush cutters for beading wire

This necklace was designed around these unusually shaped, exquisitely colored squares of purple turquoise. I made this necklace with two strands just so I could show off more of these incredible stones. I decided to use wavy sterling spacer bars on both sides of the necklace in order to have more control over the design. The spacer bars posed a challenge, though. The square turquoise beads did not fit the spacer bars, so I had to be inventive. I used Swarovski rounds to help everything fit together. I love the look of these purple turquoise squares paired up with the superb clasp, and the wavy spacer bars add extra interest. The dangles, a bit flyaway and flirty, add their own sultry impact. Don't be afraid of the design challenges an unusual material may bring. Those "problems" are your chance to shine!

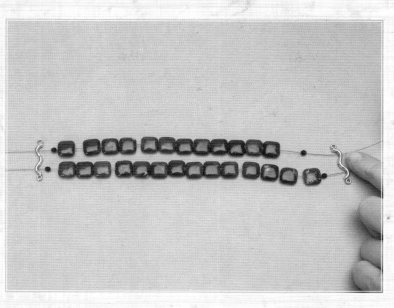

1. String necklace

Place twelve turquoise beads on the first strand of 49-strand wire and fourteen turquoise beads on the second strand of 49-strand wire. String a Purple Velvet round onto both ends of each strand. Join the two strands with spacer bars.

2. Finish stringing

String eight more turquoise beads on both sides of the shorter strand and nine more turquoise beads on both sides of the longer strand. End each strand with a barbell spacer bead, a Purple Velvet round and a barbell spacer bead. Close one side of the necklace by crimping both strands to the bar piece of the toggle clasp (see Techniques, page 19).

3. Attach clasp
Place a crimp tube and nineteen seed beads on the free end of both strands. Thread both strands through the toggle ring and back through the crimp tubes. Crimp both strands closed and trim the ends.

4. Attach dangles
Place a Purple Velvet round on a head pin and wire wrap it to the top side of a spacer bar (see Techniques, pages 16–17). Repeat on the second spacer bar. Attach the hammered silver round to the left spacer bar with a jump ring. Attach the heart-and-circle charm to the right spacer bar with a jump ring.

LACE NECKLACE

This necklace has gone from brilliant and mesmerizing in purple to
purely sensuous in neutral tones. This necklace is all about greys and
beiges. It has tons of impact even though it beckons to you softly. Where
its purple sister has sass, this necklace has class!

RESOURCES

Many of the supplies used to make the projects in this book can be found in your local craft, hobby, bead or discount department stores. If you have trouble locating a specific product, contact one of the supply sources listed below.

Aardvark Art Glass
819 E. Johnson Street
Madison, WI 53703
(608) 256-5037
www.aardvarkartglass.net

Accessories Susan
(423) 773-3619
www.accessoriessusan.com

Alicia Abla
www.aliciaabla.com

Artbeads.com
11901 137th Ave. Ct. KPN
Unit 100
Gig Harbor, WA 98329
(866) 715-2323
www.artbeads.com

Barbara Becker Simon
122 S.W. 46th Terrace
Cape Coral, FL 33914
(239) 549-5971
www.bbsimon.com

Bead 'n Shop
10/17 Vidyadhar
Nagar,
Jaipur - 302023,
Rajasthan, India
+91-141-2232165
www.beadnshop.com

The Bead Shop
158 University Ave.
Palo Alto, CA 94301
(650) 328-7925
www.beadshop.com

Brightlings Beads
1015 Aviation Parkway, Ste. 400
Morrisville, NC 27560
(919) 388-9822
www.brightlingsbeads.com

Carl Clasmeyer
(505) 989-5711
www.clasmeyer.com

Dakota Stones
7279 Washington Ave. S.
Edina, MN 55439
(866) 871-1990
www.dakotastones.com

EJR Beads
www.ejrbeads.co.uk

Fusion Beads
3830 Stone Way N.
Seattle, WA 98103
(888) 781-3559
www.fusionbeads.com

Gita Maria
(877) 247-9647
www.gitamaria.com

Green Girl Studios
(828) 298-2263
www.greengirlstudios.com

JewelrySupply.com
(916) 780-9610
www.jewelrysupply.com

Kate McKinnon
www.katemckinnon.com

Kim Miles
www.kimmiles.com

Lisa Kan Designs
www.lisakan.com

Nina Designs
(800) 336-6462
www.ninadesigns.com

Ornamentea
509 N. West St.
Raleigh, NC 27603
(919) 834-6260
www.ornamentea.com

Penny Michelle
www.pennymichelle.com

Redside Designs
www.redsidedesigns.net

The Ribbon Jar
2335 Cottage St. S.E.
Salem, OR 97302
(503) 588-7042
www.ribbonjar.com

The Ring Lord
(306) 374-1335
www.theringlord.com

Rio Grande
(800) 545-6566
www.riogrande.com

Sojourner
26 Bridge St.
Lambertville, NJ 08530
(609) 397-8849
www.sojourner.biz

Urban Maille
www.urbanmaille.com

Venetian Bead Shop
1008 Stewart Dr.
Sunnyvale, CA 94085
(800) 439-3551
www.venetianbeadshop.com

Via Murano
17654 Newhope St., Ste. A
Fountain Valley, CA 92708
(877) 842-6872
www.viamurano.com

INSPIRING ARTISTS

Letitia Baldrige Hollensteiner
Author, lecturer and "America's Leading Arbiter of Manners."
www.Letitia.com

Kate McKinnon
Artist and jewelry designer.
www.KateMcKinnon.com

Jill Newman
Polymer clay artist.
www.JustBeads.com
Seller ID: Tatercat

Margot Potter
Writer, actress, spokesperson and jewelry designer.
www.MargotPotter.com

Visit www.prettykittydogmoonjewelry.blogspot.com for Web-exclusive interviews with these talented crafters and more.

MOHS SCALE OF HARDNESS

1	TALC
2	GYPSUM
3	CALCITE
4	FLUORITE
5	APATITE
6	ORTHOCLASE
7	QUARTZ
8	TOPAZ
9	CORUNDUM
10	DIAMOND

INDEX

A

Aislyn, 62
Alice's Cosmopolitan Necklace, 28-29
Ancient Armor Bracelet, 106-109
Art House Bracelet, 104-105
Art House Earrings, 104-105
artists, inspiring, 125

B

Bead Box, 74
beading wire, 10
beads
    resources, 124
    and sundries, 12-13
bent-nose pliers, 8
Blooming Chain Maille Earrings, 62-63
Blue and Green Ruffles Necklace,
    116-117
box chain weave, 98-101
bracelets
    chain maille, 82-83, 90-93, 98-101,
    106-109
    Charming Teacup, 22-23
    Edward the Sheep, 96-97
    Gigi, 88-89
    Golden Hues, 70-71
    Nancy's Dancing Pearls, 40-41
    Naughty and Nice, 82-83
    Petals, 44-47
    Pictograph, 90-93
    Rice Jasper, 76-79
    Roses for Elizabeth, 34-37
    Ruby Coin, 76-79
    Sara Crewe, 84-87
    Sara Crewe Charm, 84-87
    Sleek Squares, 98-101
    standard sizes, 9
    Two Serendipitous, 76-79
bundled wire wrap, 18

C

Caveman Key Ring, 30-31
chain, 10
    finding center, 60

chain maille patterns, 32-33, 38-39, 62-
    63, 72-73, 82-83, 90-93, 98-101,
    102-103, 106-109
chain-nose pliers, 8
Charming Teacup Bracelet, 22-23
Charming Teacup Earrings, 22-23
choker
    Diamond, 102-103
    Mother's Love Pin and, 24-25
Citrus Gumdrop Earrings, 56-57
Citrus Gumdrop Necklace, 56-57
clasps, 11
Color, 114
    experimenting with, 56
    garnets, 58
components. See findings
Creative Challenges, 37, 55, 64, 85,
    101, 111, 116
Creative Connections, 31, 35, 62,
    68, 80
crimp tubes, 11, 19

D

Delicate Earrings, 60-61
Delicate Necklace, 60-61
Diamond Choker, 102-103

E

earrings
    Art House, 104-105
    Blooming Chain Maille,
    62-63
    Charming Teacup, 22-23
    Citrus Gumdrop, 56-57
    Delicate, 60-61
    Elegant Underwater, 26-27
    Golden Flowers, 110-113
    Golden Hues, 70-71
    Hip Chicks, 32-33
    Looping Deco, 110-113
    Magnificent Mineral, 50-51
    Mandala, 94-95
    Naughty and Nice, 82-83
    On-the-Square, 110-113

Pictograph, 90-93
Roses for Elizabeth, 34-37
Sara Crewe, 84-87
Spice Market, 66-67
Spiral, 58-59
Trinity Spiral, 64-65
Trio of Sparkling, 110-113
Turning Leaf, 52-55
Vines, 44-47
Eclipse Necklace, 118-119
Edward the Sheep Bracelet, 96-97
Electric Purple Necklace, 120-123
Elegant Underwater Earrings, 26-27

F

Fairy in the Garden Necklace, 68-69
Family and Friends, 20
findings, 11
flat-nose pliers, 8
flush cutters, 9

G

garnet, various colors, 58
Gerlach, Elizabeth King, 35
Gigi Bracelet, 88-89
Golden Flowers Earrings, 110-113
Golden Hues Bracelet, 70-71
Golden Hues Earrings, 70-71

H

head pins, 11
    wire wrapping on, 16-17
Hip Chicks Earrings, 32-33

I

Indian Summer Necklace, 72-73

J

jewelry, nontraditional materials, 12
jump rings, 11
    heavy gauge, 72
    working with, 14-15

K

key ring, 30-31

L

Lace Necklace, 120-124
lampwork, 22-23, 30-31, 34-37, 68-69, 84-87, 90-93, 104-105, 116-117
lariat, 50-51
Looping Deco Earrings, 110-113
Lybarger, Cathy, 31

M

Magnificent Mineral Earrings, 50-51
Magnificent Mineral Lariat, 50-51
Mandala Earrings, 94-95
materials, 8-13
measuring tape, 9
memory wire, 10
Miles, Kim, 68
minerals, scale of hardness, 125
Mohs scale of hardness, 125
Mother's Love Pin and Choker, 24-25
multi-strand attachments, 11

N

Nancy's Dancing Pearls Bracelet, 40-41
Nature, 42
Naughty and Nice Bracelet, 82-83
Naughty and Nice Earrings, 82-83
necklaces. *See also* choker, lariat
    Alice's Cosmopolitan, 28-29
    Blue and Green Ruffles, 116-117
    Citrus Gumdrop, 56-57
    Delicate, 60-61
    Eclipse, 118-119
    Electric Purple, 120-123
    Fairy in the Garden, 68-69
    Indian Summer, 72-73
    Lace Necklace, 120-124
    Portrait of Nature, 48-49
    Rainbow Ruffles, 116-117
    Red Planet, 80-81
    Sara Crewe, 84-87
    standard sizes, 9
    Sun and Shadow, 118-119
    Treasured Friends, 38-39
    Trinity Spiral, 64-65

O

On-the-Square Earrings, 110-113

P

Petals and Vines Bracelet and Earrings, 44-47
Pictograph Bracelet, 90-93
Pictograph Earrings, 90-93
pin, 24-25
pliers, 8
Portrait of Nature Necklace, 48-49

R

Rainbow Ruffles Necklace, 116-117
Ralph, Emma, 80
Red Planet Necklace, 80-81
resources, 124
ribbon
    choker, 24-25
    tying with, 88-89
Rice Jasper Bracelet, 76, 79
rosary pliers. *see* round-nose pliers
Roses for Elizabeth Bracelet, 34-37
Roses for Elizabeth Earrings, 34-37
round-nose pliers, 8
rubber rings, 102-103
Ruby Coin Bracelet, 76-78
ruler, 9

S

Sara Crewe Bracelet, 84-87
Sara Crewe Charm Bracelet, 84-87
Sara Crewe Earrings, 84-87
Sara Crewe Necklace, 84-87
scissors, 9
Sleek Squares Bracelet, 98-101
Spice Market Earrings, 66-67
Spiral Earrings, 58-59
stringing materials, 10
Sun and Shadow Necklace, 118-119

T

techniques, 14-19
Tips, 8, 24, 26, 28, 30, 32, 38, 40, 44, 48, 52, 56, 58, 60, 70, 72, 82, 98, 102

tools, 8-9
Treasured Friends Necklace, 38-39
Trinity Spiral Earrings, 64-65
Trinity Spiral Necklace, 64-65
Trio of Sparkling Earrings, 110-113
Turning Leaf Earrings, 52-55
Two Serendipitous Bracelets, 76-79

V

Vines Earrings, 44-47

W

wire, 10
wire straighteners, 9
wire wrapping, 16-18

INDULGE YOUR CREATIVE SIDE WITH THESE NORTH LIGHT TITLES

Sparkletastic
Margot Potter
The time has come for you to break out the glitter and release your inner diva! *Sparkletastic* gives you over 40 fabulous jewelry pieces and accessories to wear when you want to sparkle. From outrageous lunch-boxes to an over-the-top crystal tiara and matching necklace, this book has a dizzying array of designs that are fun, quick and easy to make. Get ready for a glamorous adventure to a glittery wonderland. Viva la sparkle!
ISBN-10: 1-58180-973-2
ISBN-13: 978-1-58180-973-2
paperback
128 pages
Z0759

Simply Beautiful Beaded Jewelry
Heidi Boyd
Author and designer Heidi Boyd has filled this fabulous jewelry book to the brim with over 50 gorgeous beaded necklaces, bracelets, earrings and accessories. Her trademark style shines in each of the projects and variations. Best of all, every piece is simple to make and beautiful to wear. Even a beginning crafter can easily finish any project in the book in one afternoon. The book includes a helpful techniques section and insightful tips scattered throughout.
ISBN-10: 1-58180-774-0
ISBN-13: 978-1-58180-774-5
paperback
128 pages
33445

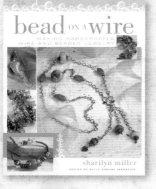

Bead on a Wire
Sharilyn Miller
In her latest book, magazine editor and popular author Sharilyn Miller shows crafters of all levels how to get in on the popularity of jewelry and beading. Inside *Bead on a Wire*, you'll find an in-depth section on design and construction techniques that make it a snap to get started. You'll love to make the 20 step-by-step bead and wire jewelry projects, including gorgeous earrings, necklaces, brooches and bracelets. You'll be amazed at how easy it is to start making fashionable jewelry that's guaranteed to inspire compliments.
ISBN-10: 1-58180-650-7
ISBN-13: 978-1-58180-650-2
paperback
128 pages
33239

The Impatient Beader
Margot Potter
If you're creative but lack time, focus or motivation, *The Impatient Beader* is the book for you. Author Margot Potter guides you through over 50 sassy jewelry projects, from the sweet to the outright sizzling. You can finish each of the projects in just a few easy steps, and a skill level guide lets you know what you're getting into before you get going. An easy-to-follow techniques section shows you everything you need to get your bead on, and cartoon Margot pops up every few pages to give you tips on how to become a beading goddess.
ISBN-10: ISBN 1-58180-762-7
ISBN-13: 978-1-58180-762-2
paperback
128 pages
33431

These and other fine North Light titles are available at your favorite local craft retailer or bookstore or online supplier.